생활 속의 참선수행 Practice In Daily Life ⑫

Finding A Way Forward:
A Gift for Mothers and Children

잘 돼야 돼!

잘 돼야 돼!
대행큰스님 법문
생활 속의 참선수행 ⑫ / 한영합본

발행일	2016년 7월 초판1쇄
	2016년 8월 초판2쇄
영문번역	한마음국제문화원
표지디자인	박수연
편집	한마음국제문화원
발행	한마음출판사
출판등록	384-2000-000010
전화	031-470-3175
팩스	031-470-3209
이메일	onemind@hanmaum.org

© 2016(재)한마음선원
본 출판물은 저작권법에 의하여 보호를 받는 저작물이므로
무단 복제와 무단 전재를 할 수 없습니다.

Finding A Way Forward: A Gift for Mothers and Children
Practice in Daily Life ⑫ / Bilingual, Korean·English
Dharma Talks by Seon Master Daehaeng

First Edition First Print: July 2016
First Edition Second Print: August 2016
English Translation by
Hanmaum International Culture Institute
Edited by Hanmaum International Culture Institute
Cover Design by Su Yeon Park
Published by Hanmaum Publications
www.hanmaumbooks.org

© 2016 Hanmaum Seonwon Foundation
All rights reserved, including the right to reproduce
this work in any form.

Printed in the Republic of Korea

ISBN 978-89-91857-42-1 (04220) / 978-89-951830-0-7 (set)

국립중앙도서관 출판예정도서목록(CIP)

잘 돼야 돼! = Finding a way forward : a gift for mothers and children : 한영합본 / 대행큰스님 법문 ; 영문번역: 한마음국제문화원. -- [안양] : 한마음출판사, 2016
  p. ; cm. -- (생활 속의 참선 수행 =Practice in daily life ; 12)

한영대역본임
ISBN 978-89-91857-42-1 04220 : ₩6000
ISBN 978-89-951830-0-7 (세트) 04220

설법[說法]
법문(불경)[法文]

225.2-KDC6
294.34-DDC23   CIP2016012129

A CIP catalogue record of the National Library of Korea for this book is available at the homepage of CIP(http://seoji.nl.go.kr) and Korean Library Information System Network(http://www.nl.go.kr/kolisnet). (CIP2016012129)

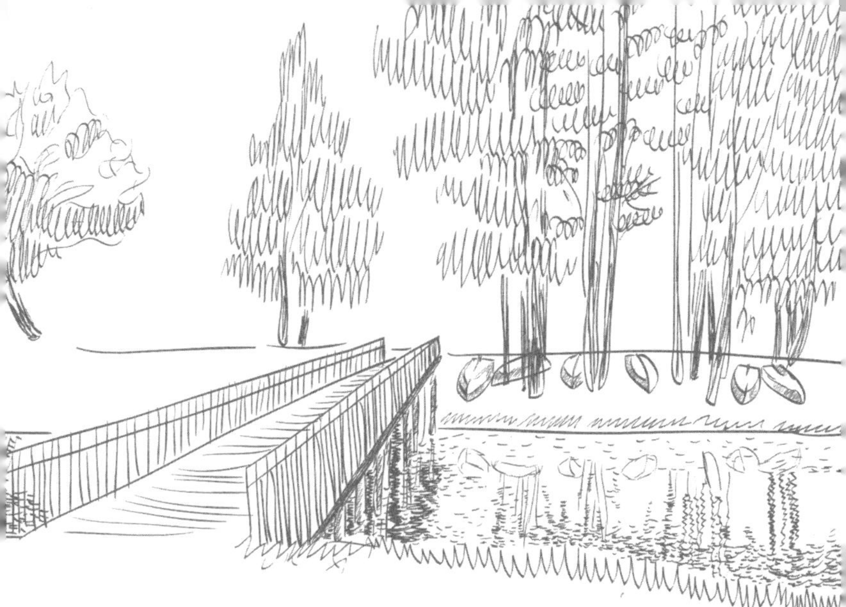

A Gift for Mothers and Children
Finding A Way Forward

Seon Master Daehaeng

잘 돼야 돼!

대행큰스님 법문

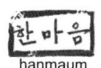

차례

10 머리글

12 대행큰스님에 대하여

24 잘 돼야 돼!

Contents

11   Foreword

13   About Daehaeng Kun Sunim

25   Finding A Way Forward:
          A Gift for Mothers and Children

천지 만물 모든 생명

천지 만물 모든 생명 너와 함께 있으니
유정무정 화합하여 한마음을 이루면
언제나 어디서나 내 몸 아님이 없나니
모든 것 내 한생각에 모두 움직이리라.
모든 것 내 한생각에 모두 움직이리라.

부처와 더불어 일체 만물 만생이
모두가 공했으니 공하여 평등하면
열반이자 부처요 한생각을 냈다 하면
그대로가 법이며 움직이는 용이라.
그대로가 법이며 움직이는 용이라.

-대행큰스님 게송 중에서

Everything in the World

All beings and everything in the world
are all together with me.
If I can combine the seen and unseen,
and become one mind,
wherever I go,
everything I meet, everyone I meet,
is also my body.
And from this all-together-place,
the thoughts I raise move everything.
The thoughts I raise move everything.

Buddhas and every life and thing,
are all empty, ceaselessly changing.
If you realize this emptiness,
if you truly realize that everything
is yourself,
this is nirvana, this is Buddha.
And from this state,
a single thought will become reality,
a single thought will move and work in the world.
A single thought will become reality,
a single thought will move and work in the world.

– Daehaeng

머리글

대행큰스님이 지난 50여 년 동안 끊임없이 중생들에게 베풀어주신 수많은 법문이 있었지만, 핵심을 짚어내는 하나의 단어가 있다면, 그건 아마도 "참나"일 것입니다. 항상 나와 함께 있어서 보지 못하는 내 안의 진짜 나, 그 "참나"를 발견하여 당당하고 싱그럽게 살아가기를 바라는, 중생을 위한 스님의 간절한 바램은 이 한 편의 법문 속에도 여지없이 드러나 있습니다.

누구에게나 내면에는 만물만생을 다 먹여 살리고도 되남는 마음속 한 점의 불씨가 있습니다. 그 영원한 불씨를 찾아 광대무변한 마음법의 이치를 체득하여, 진정한 자유인으로서, 우주의 한 일원으로서 당당히 그 역할을 해나가길 바라는 대행큰스님의 간곡한 뜻이 이 법문을 통해 여러분 모두의 마음에 전해지길 바랍니다.

한마음국제문화원 일동 합장

Foreword

Over the last fifty years, Daehaeng Kun Sunim gave countless Dharma talks and teachings to beings without number, but if all those talks could be summed up into one word, it would be "true self."

This true essence has always been with us, yet remains unseen. Discover it for yourself, and in doing so, learn to live with courage, dignity, and joy. That all beings should awaken to this true essence is Daehaeng Kun Sunim's deepest wish. When you've tasted the purest and most refreshing spring water imaginable, you naturally want to share it with others.

Within us all is this seed, this spark that feeds and sustains each and every being. Discover this eternal spark and realize its profound and unlimited ability. If you can do this, you'll know what it means to truly be a free person, and you can fulfill the great role that is yours as a member of the whole universe.

With palms together,
The Hanmaum International Culture Institute

대행큰스님에 대하여

　　대행큰스님께서는 여러 면에서 매우 보기 드문 선사(禪師)셨다. 무엇보다 선사라면 당연히 비구 스님을 떠올리는 전통 속에서 여성으로서 선사가 되셨으며, 비구 스님들을 제자로 두었던 유일한 비구니 스님이셨고, 노년층 여성이 주된 신도계층을 이루었던 한국 불교에 젊은 세대의 청장년층 남녀들을 대거 참여하게 만들어 한국불교에 새로운 풍격(風格)을 일으키는데 일조한 큰 스승이셨다. 또한 전통 비구니 강원과 비구니 종단에 대한 지속적인 지원을 펼치심으로써 비구니 승단을 발전시키는데 중추적인 역할을 하셨다.

　　큰스님께서는 어느 누구나 마음수행을 통해 깨달을 수 있음을 강조하시면서 삭발제자와 유발제자를 가리지 않고 법을 구하는 이들에게는 모두 똑같이 가르침을 주셨다.

　　스님은 1927년 서울에서 태어나 일찍이 9세경에 자성을 밝히셨고 당신이 증득(證得)하신 바를 완성하기 위해 오랫동안 산중에서 수행하셨다. 훗날, 누더기가 다 된 해진 옷을 걸치고 손에 주어지는 것만을 먹으며 지냈던 그 당시를 회상하며 스님은 의도적으로 고행을

About Daehaeng Kun Sunim

Daehaeng *Kun Sunim*[1] (1927-2012) was a rare teacher in Korea: a female *Seon(Zen)*[2] master, a nun whose students included monks as well as nuns, and a teacher who helped revitalize Korean Buddhism by dramatically increasing the participation of young people and men. She broke out of traditional models of spiritual practice to teach in such a way that allowed anyone to practice and awaken, making laypeople a particular focus of her efforts. At the same time, she was a major force for the advancement of *Bhikkunis*,[3] heavily supporting traditional nuns' colleges as well as the modern Bhikkuni Council of Korea.

---

1. Sunim / Kun Sunim: Sunim is the respectful title of address for a Buddhist monk or nun in Korea, and Kun Sunim is the title given to outstanding nuns or monks.

2. Seon(禪)(Chan, Zen)**:** Seon describes the unshakeable state where one has firm faith in their inherent foundation, their Buddha-nature, and so returns everything they encounter back to this fundamental mind. It also means letting go of "I," "me," and "mine" throughout one's daily life.

3. Bhikkunis: Female sunims who are fully ordained are called Bhikkuni(比丘尼) sunims, while male sunims who are fully ordained are called Bhikku(比丘) sunims. This can also be a polite way of indicating male or female sunims.

하고자 했던 것이 아니라 당신에게 주어진 환경이 그러했노라고, 또한 근본 불성자리에 일체를 맡기고 그 맡긴 일이 어떻게 작용하는지를 관하는 일에 완전히 몰두하고 있었기에 다른 것에는 신경을 쓸 틈이 없었노라고 말씀하셨다.

그 시절의 체험이 스님의 가르치는 방식을 형성하는데 깊은 영향을 미쳤다. 스님은 우리가 본래부터 어마어마한 잠재력을, 무궁무진한 에너지와 지혜를 가지고 있는데도 대부분이 그 역량을 알지 못해 끊임없이 많은 고통을 겪으며 살고 있음을 절실히 느끼며 안타까워하셨다. 우리들 각자 안에 존재하는 이 위대한 빛을 명백히 알고 있었기에, 스님은 본래부터 가지고 있는 근본자성(自性)인 참나를 믿고 의지해 살라 가르치셨고, 이 중요한 진리에서 벗어나는 그 어떤 것도 가르치기를 단호히 거부하셨다.

의도한 바는 아니셨지만, 스님은 매일매일의 일상 속에서 누구나 내면에 갖추어 가지고 있는 근본이자 진수(眞髓)인 참나와 진정으로 통할 수 있게 되었을 때 어떠한 일이 일어나는 지를 역력히 보여 주셨다. 사람들은 스님 곁에 있을 때 자신들을 무한히 받아주고 품어주는 것만 같은, 말로 형언키 어려운 정밀(靜謐)한 기운을 느꼈고, 스님이 다른 사람들을 도와줄 때 드러내 보이는 깊은 법력 또한 목도하곤 하였다. 하지만 이 모든 일들은 당신

Born in Seoul, Korea, she awakened when she was around eight years old and spent the years that followed learning to put her understanding into practice. For years, she wandered the mountains of Korea, wearing ragged clothes and eating only what was at hand. Later, she explained that she hadn't been pursuing some type of asceticism; rather, she was just completely absorbed in entrusting everything to her fundamental *Buddha*[4] essence and observing how that affected her life.

Those years profoundly shaped Kun Sunim's later teaching style; she intimately knew the great potential, energy, and wisdom inherent within each of us, and recognized that most of the people she encountered suffered because they didn't realize this about themselves. Seeing clearly the great light in every individual, she taught people to rely upon this inherent foundation, and refused to teach anything that distracted from this most important truth.

Without any particular intention to do so, Daehaeng Kun Sunim demonstrated on a daily basis the freedom and ability that arises when

---

4. Buddha: In this text, "Buddha" and "Bodhisattva" are capitalized out of respect, because these represent the essence and function of the enlightened mind. "The Buddha" always refers to Sakyamuni Buddha.

자신을 돋보이게 하거나 과시하려 했던 게 아니었다. 사실 스님께서는 당신의 법력을 늘 감추려고 하셨다. 마음공부의 목적이 놀라운 능력을 갖게 되는 것이 아님에도 대중들이 그것에만 집착하게 되는 폐단을 우려하셨기 때문이었다.

그렇지만 당신이 하신 모든 일을 통해, 우리가 내면에 있는 참나와 진정으로 하나가 되었을 때 그 능력과 자유로움이 어떤 것인지를 보여 주셨다. 스님은 우리 모두가 근본을 통해 연결되어 있으므로 다 통할 수 있고, 그럼으로써 서로 깊이 이해할 수 있다는 것을 보여주셨으며, 더 나아가 우리가 근본자리에서 일으키는 한생각이 이 세상에 법이 되어 돌아갈 수 있다는 것도 보여 주셨다.

어떤 의미에서는 이 모든 일이 우리가 만물만생과 정말로 하나가 되었을 때 자연스레 부수적으로 나오는 것이라고 할 수 있다. 상대를 둘로 보거나 방해물로 여기는 마음이 사라졌을 때, 진정으로 모두와 조화롭게 흘러갈 수 있게 되었을 때 이 모든 일이 가능할 수 있게 되는 것이다. 이렇게 되면, 다가오는 상대가 누구든 별개의 존재로 느끼지 않게 된다. 그들이 또 다른 우리 자신들의 모습이기 때문이다. 일체가 둘이 아님을 뼛속 깊이 느끼는 사람이, 어찌 자신 앞에 닥친 인연을 나 몰라라 하고 등져 버릴 수 있겠는가?

we truly connect with this fundamental essence inherent within us. The sense of acceptance and connection people felt from being around her, as well as the abilities she manifested, weren't things she was trying to show off. In fact, she usually tried to hide them because people would tend to cling to these, without realizing that chasing after them cannot lead to either freedom or awakening.

Nonetheless, in her very life, in everything she did, she demonstrated the freedom and ability that arises when we truly connect with this very basic, fundamental essence that we all have – that we are. She showed that because we are all interconnected, we can deeply understand what's going on with others, and that the intentions we give rise to can manifest and function in the world.

All of these are in a sense side effects, things that arise naturally when we are truly one with everyone and everything around us. They happen because we are able to flow in harmony with our world, with no dualistic views or attachments to get in the way. At this point, other beings are not cut off from us; they are another shape of ourselves. Who, feeling this to their very bones, could turn their back on others?

스님은 중생들이 가지고 오는 어려운 문제나 상황들을 해결할 수 있도록 도와주셨으며, 이러한 스님의 자비로운 원력은 당신이 도시로 나와 본격적으로 대중들을 가르치기 이전에 이미 한국에서는 전설이 되어 있었다. 1950년대 말경, 치악산 상원사 근처 한 움막에서 수행차 몇년 간 머무르신 적이 있었는데, 그 소문을 듣고 전국에서 찾아오는 사람들이 끊이질 않았다. 차마 그들의 고통스런 호소를 내칠수가 없었던 스님은 일일이 그들의 말에 귀기울이며 마음을 다해 그들을 도와주셨다. 스님은 자비를 물 마른 웅덩이에서 죽어가는 물고기를 살리는 방생에 비유하셨다. 집세가 없어 셋집에서 쫓겨난 사람들에게 집을 마련해 주고, 학비가 없어서 학교를 마칠 수 없는 학생들에게 학비를 대주셨지만, 스님의 자비행(慈悲行)을 아는 사람은 손을 꼽을 정도밖에 되지 않았다.

　　그러나 문제를 해결해 주면 그때뿐 또 다른 문제가 닥쳐오면 속수무책이 되어 버리고 마는 사람들을 보며, 스님께서는 중생들이 자신의 문제를 스스로 해결하고 윤회(輪廻)[1]의 굴레에서

---

1. 윤회(輪廻): 산스크리트어의 삼사라(samsara)를 번역한 말로 쉼없이 돈다는 생사의 바퀴를 뜻함. 다시 말해, 수레바퀴가 끊임없이 구르는 것과 같이, 중생이 번뇌와 업에 의하여 삼계(三界: 색계, 욕계, 무색계) 육도(六道: 지옥, 아귀, 축생, 아수라, 인간, 천상)라는 생사의 세계를 그치지 않고 돌고 도는 현상을 일컬음.

It was this deep compassion that made her a legend in Korea long before she formally started teaching. She was known for having the spiritual power to help people in all circumstances and with every kind of problem. She compared compassion to freeing a fish from a drying puddle, putting a homeless family into a home, or providing the school fees that would allow a student to finish high school. And when she did things like this, and much more, few knew that she was behind it.

Her compassion was also unconditional. She would offer what help she could to individuals and organizations, whether they be Christian or Buddhist, a private organization or governmental. She would help nun's temples that had no relationship with her temple, Christian organizations that helped look after children living on their own, city-run projects to help care for the elderly, and much, much more. Yet, even when she provided material support, always there was the deep, unseen aid she offered through this connection we all share.

However, she saw that ultimately, for people to live freely and go forward in the world as a blessing to all around them, they needed to know

벗어나 자유인이 될 수 있는 도리를 가르치는 일이 더 시급함을 느끼셨다. 누구나가 다 가지고 있는 참나, 이 내면의 밝디밝은 진수(眞髓)를 알게 하여, 자신들이 자유롭게 사는 것은 물론이요, 자신들의 삶이 인연 맺은 모든 이에게 축복이 되어 이 한 세상을 활달이 살아갈 수 있도록 해야겠다고 다짐하셨다.

 마침내 산에서 내려온 스님께서는 1972년 경기도 안양에 한마음선원을 설립하셨다. 이후 40여 년 동안 한마음선원에 주석하시며, 지혜를 원하는 자에게 지혜를, 배고프고 가난한 자에게는 먹을 것과 물질을, 아파하는 자에게는 치유의 방편을 내어주시는 무한량의 자비를 베푸시며 불법의 진리를 가르쳐 주셨다. 스님은 도움이 필요한 다양한 사회복지 프로그램을 후원하셨고, 6개국에 10개의 해외지원과 국내 15개의 지원을 세우셨다. 또한 스님의 가르침은 영어, 독어, 스페인어, 러시아어, 중국어, 일본어, 불어, 이태리어, 베트남어, 인도네시아어, 아랍어 등으로 번역 출간되었다. 스님은 2012년 5월 21일 자정, 세납 86세로 입적하셨으며, 법랍 63세셨다.

about this bright essence that is within each of us. To help people discover this for themselves, she founded the first *Hanmaum*[5] Seon Center in 1972. For the next forty years she gave wisdom to those who needed wisdom, food and money to those who were poor and hungry, and compassion to those who were hurting.

---

5. Hanmaum[han-ma-um]**:** "Han" means one, great, and combined, while "maum" means mind, as well as heart, and together they mean everything combined and connected as one. What is called "Hanmaum" is intangible, unseen, and transcends time and space. It has no beginning or end, and is sometimes called our fundamental mind. It also means the mind of all beings and everything in the universe connected and working together as one. In English, we usually translate this as "one mind."

본 저서는 대행큰스님의 법문을
한국어와 영어 합본 시리즈로 출간하는
〈생활 속의 참선수행〉시리즈 제12권으로써
2001년 3월 4일 정기법회 때 설하신 내용을
재편집한 것입니다.

This Dharma talk was given by
Daehaeng Kun Sunim on Sunday, March 4, 2001. This is
Volume 12 in the ongoing series,
Practice in Daily Life.

Daehaeng Kun Sunim founded ten overseas branches of Hanmaum Seon Center, and her teachings have been translated into twelve different languages to date: English, German, Russian, Chinese, French, Spanish, Indonesian, Italian, Japanese, Vietnamese, Estonian, and Arabic, in addition to the original Korean. For more information about these or the overseas centers, please see the back of this book.

잘 돼야 돼!

2001년 3월 4일

여러분들과 같이 이렇게 한자리를 하면서 가만히 생각해 보니 옛날에 봤던 일이 기억납니다. 다람쥐가 고구마밭을 온통 그냥 다 파서 재끼고, 그 고구마를 전부 훔쳐 가는 걸 봤거든요. 그랬는데 말이에요, 그 다람쥐가 어떻게 큰 고구마를 가지고 가나 하고 보니까 그거를 돌에다가 굴려서 올려놓고는 이마에다 대고선 딱 붙잡으니깐 아, 딱 붙잡아지잖아요. 근데 그렇게 해 가지고 뛰어요. 그거 혼자 보기는 정말 아까웠습니다.

왜 이 다람쥐 얘기를 하느냐 하면 동물이 사는 세상이나, 사람이 사는 세상이나 가만히 보면 크게 다르지 않아서입니다. 역경이 닥쳤을 때 지혜롭게 해결해 볼 생각도 안하고 그냥 사는 아주 못난 사람보다 저 고구마 이고 가는 다람쥐가 더 훌륭하다는 생각이 들어서요.

Finding A Way Forward:
A Gift for Mothers and Children

March 4, 2001

Sitting here together with you, I'm reminded of a funny thing I saw a long time ago. One day, I saw a chipmunk digging in a small patch of sweet potatoes and stealing them. When I first saw him, it was obvious he was trying to dig up the sweet potatoes, but I was curious what he would do once he got one. So I sat there and watched him.

He would dig up a sweet potato, push it onto a flat rock at the edge of the patch, and using that as a platform, he would grab the sides of the sweet potato, put his forehead on it, and then, pushing with his head, would run away carrying the sweet potato on his head. It was so fun to watch!

The reason I mention this story is because there isn't a huge difference between the animal world and the human world. I think a chipmunk that can figure out how to carry away sweet

모습만 달랐다뿐이지 사는 게 뭐가 다르겠습니까? 부처님이 허공에 꽉 차 지혜와 깨달음이 가득하더라도 여러분이 없다면, 여러분이 그것을 얻고자 하는 마음이 없다면 부처님이 꽉 차기는커녕 아무 것도 없을 겁니다.

근데 여러분이 계시기 때문에, 여러분이 그것을 구하고자 하는 간절함이 있기 때문에 부처님이 허공에 꽉 찼다는 거죠. 그러니 딴 데, 딴 세상에 부처님이 계신 줄 알지 마시고 여러분 가까이, 여러분 계신 데 계시다는 걸 아주 뚜렷하게 아셨으면 좋겠습니다.

우리가 한 가족으로 살면서도 무슨 일이 생기면 서로 원망을 하고 화목하게 지내지 못할 때가 많아요. 모두 남의 탓이라고 생각을 하게 되고 내 탓은 하나도 없고요. 상대방의 탓으로만 돌릴 때가 많죠.

potatoes is much more impressive than a human being who just sits in the middle of his problems without trying to figure out how to wisely overcome them.

Animals and people have different appearances, but the essentials of how we go about our lives are the same. Even though Buddhas, enlightenment, and wisdom fill the air, if you weren't here, trying to find them and become a fully developed human being, it would be as if they didn't exist at all.

After you've been born into this world, and begun to practice with the utmost diligence, you can realize that Buddhas inherently fill the air around us. So don't look for Buddha somewhere far away from you; Buddha is always right where you are. I hope that you all will come to deeply know this for yourselves.

Just because you exist, you'll encounter all kinds of things, but how you react to them determines what happens next. Even in our own family, we sometimes blame and resent each other. We're convinced that everything is someone else's fault, and that we're the victims of it all.

하지만 따지고 보면 잘했든 못했든 각자 자기가 있기 때문에 그 모든 게 벌어졌다는 걸 아실 거예요. 남의 탓할 게 하나도 없어요. 그걸 정확히 안다면 우리가 몸을 끌고 돌아 댕기면서 구경하고 이러지 않고도, 몸을 가지고 그렇게 애쓰지 않아도 살 수는 있지 않나 싶습니다. 더 나아가 굳이 이 세상에 몸을 갖고 나오지 않아도 되고요.

찰나찰나 우리가 보고 듣고 하는 그거를 가만히 생각해 보십시오. 우리가 매사 함이 있이 살고 있는 게 아닙니다. 그게 자연스러운 거예요. 그러니깐 모두가 공했다고 했죠. 그거 한번 잘 생각해 보세요. 여러분이 발자취 없는 걸음걸이처럼 함이 없이 살아가신다면 이렇게까지 고통을 받고 이러는 게 없어질 겁니다. 왜냐하면 서로 근본으로 다 연결되어 돌아가고 있기 때문에 '내가 했다'라고 할 게 없으니까 걸릴 게 없어서예요.

However, when you examine things closely, you'll find that you played a role in all of it. At a very fundamental level, just because you exist, you are feeling and going through those things. There's no use blaming others; it's all something you had a hand in.

If you can thoroughly understand this, then you can take care of everything through *mind*,[6] instead of trying to solve things by dragging your body around here and there. At this point, it won't be necessary to be reborn with a body.

In fact, look at the way we're already living. Everything we do, see, and hear passes by in an instant. It unfolds naturally, without us trying to control it or let it go. It just flows and changes naturally. This is why it's said that everything is empty.

Please take some time to seriously reflect upon this. If you can flow like this, taking care of things wisely while letting go of thoughts along the lines of "I did" or "This (thing) happened to

---

6. Mind(心)(Kor. –maum)**:** In Mahayana Buddhism, "mind" refers to this fundamental mind, and almost never means the brain or intellect. It is intangible, beyond space and time, and has no beginning or end. It is the source of everything, and everyone is endowed with it.

주인공(主人空)²에다 모든 거를 맡겨 놓고 사시라 이렇게 말했던 것도 여러분들이 이거 해야겠다 저거 해야겠다, 이거 원망하고 저거 원망하고, 이것 저것 생각하느라 사는 재미가 없이 살아서지요. 그렇게 살면 얼마나 힘들겠습니까? 어디 그게 사람 사는 겁니까? 저 건너 보이는 산이 내 정원이 되기도 하고 그래서 내가 웃고 거길 갈 수 있고 그래야 되겠죠.

좀 이상스럽게 생각할 수 있는 얘기를 하나 하겠습니다. 어느 선지식(善知識)³이 병원에 가서 다리 수술을 하려니 몹시 아플 것 같더랍니다. 그래서 육신은 거기다 놔두고 자기는 산으로 올라갔는데, 올라가서 얼마 있다 보니 깨어나시라고 누가 자꾸 건드리더랍니다. 그래서 시간이 됐나 보다 하고는 얼른 자기 몸으로 다시 들어가 보니 수술이 다 끝나 있더래요. 그래서 그 아픈 걸 면했답니다.

---

2. 주인공(主人空): 우리 모두 스스로 갖추어 가지고 있는 근본마음으로 일체 만물만생의 근본과 직결된 자리. 나를 존재하게 하고, 나를 움직이게 하며, 내 모든 것을 관장하는 참 주인이므로 주인(主人)이며, 매 순간 쉴 사이 없이 변하고 돌아가 고정된 실체가 없으므로 빌 공(空)자를 써서, 주인공(主人空)이라 함.

3. 선지식(善知識): 불법의 진리를 가르쳐 주며, 사람들을 바른 길로 이끌어주는 훌륭한 지도자 혹은 현자(賢者)를 뜻함.

me," then the pain and hardships of your life will also naturally flow away. Once we let go of "I," there's no place for any of those things to remain.

I've told you to entrust everything to your foundation, *Juingong*,[7] because, frankly, life becomes plodding drudgery when you're always worrying about having to do this or that, hating others, resenting them, or trying to think your way through every situation. Is this really the best we can do? No! While sitting here taking care of everything, you should also be able to laugh and go for a walk on that mountain in the far distance.

Let me give you an example. This story may seem a bit strange, but bear with me. A man who had awakened needed surgery on his leg, and this was expected to be quite painful. So, when the time came, he left his body behind in the operating room and went to relax in the

---

7. Juingong(主人空): Pronounced "ju-in-gong." Juin (主人) means the true doer or the master, and gong (空) means "empty." Thus Juingong is our true nature, our true essence, the master within that is always changing and manifesting, without a fixed form or shape.

Daehaeng Sunim has compared Juingong to the root of the tree. Our bodies and consciousness are like the branches and leaves, but it is the root that is the source of the tree, and it is the root that sustains the visible tree.

이런 애기는 직접 경험을 해 보지 않고는 이해하기가 힘드시겠지만 우스개로 그냥 하는 말이 아닙니다. 이 공부를 깊이 하다 보면 별별 경험을 다 하게 되는데 이런 걸 어찌 말로 새록새록이 다 할 수 있겠습니까? 사람 사는데 벌어지는 일들을 단정 지어서 몇 마디로 할 수가 없죠. 아니, 한마디도 할 수가 없어요. 그건 귀정지어 놓은 일이 아니기 때문입니다. 가다가도 생기는 일이기 때문이죠. 예를 들어 가다가 뗏목이 걸쳐서 가로막고 있으면 그냥 한다 안 한다도 없이 그거 치우고 갈 거 아닙니까!

　　부처님의 마음[4]법은 만물만생이 서로 근본으로 통해 있어 그 마음이 보살(菩薩)[5]의 응신으로서 나투어 대신하는 거죠. 그리고 그렇게 응신으로서 하는 법은, 여러분이 통신을 했을 때 이렇다, 저렇다 하는 건 아주 큰 법에서 결정이 되는 거에요.

---

4. 마음: 단순히 두뇌를 통한 정신활동이나 지성을 일컫는 말이 아니라, 만물만생이 지니고 있으며, 일체만법을 움직이게 하는 천지의 근본을 뜻함. '안에 있다, 밖에 있다' 혹은, '이거다 저거다'라고 말할 수 없으며 시작과 끝이 없고 사라질 수도 파괴될 수도 없음. 시공을 초월하여 존재함.

5. 보살(菩薩): 위로는 불법을 닦아 깨달음의 지혜를 얻고, 아래로는 중생을 구제하며 그들이 스스로 깨닫도록 도와주는 부처의 화현.

mountains. After a while he noticed that someone was touching him and trying to wake him up. So he returned to his body, and the surgery was already finished. In this way, he avoided the severe pain of the surgery.

This story may seem kind of hard to accept if you haven't experienced this for yourself, but I'm telling you about this for a reason. As your practice of letting go and relying upon your foundation becomes deeper, you will go through innumerable strange and weird experiences. It's not remotely possible for me to describe them all. How could a few words grasp this flowing that is life? If you're walking along and you find something blocking your way, you move it or go around. You just do this and continue on.

I've told you that when you unconditionally entrust something to your foundation, it responds to that because everything shares the same

---

8. Bodhisattva(菩薩)**:** A Bodhisattva is traditionally thought of as an awakened being who remains in this realm in order to continue helping those who are suffering. However, in the most basic sense, a Bodhisattva is the manifestation of our inherent, enlightened essence that is working to save beings, and which uses the non-dual wisdom of enlightenment to help them awaken for themselves.

그렇지만 우리들이 살림하면서 마주치는 일상생활에서의 많은 일들은 결정짓지 않고 그냥 함이 없이 하시는 것이 제일입니다. 그래서 주인공에다 모든 걸, 잘하는 것도 못하는 것도 놓고 하시라, 구정물 들어오는 것도 맑은 물 들어오는 것도 탓하지 마시고, 내가 사용할 수 있는 그 물로 바꿔 쓰시라 이렇게 말씀 드리죠.

이것을 어떻게 자세히 말을 해야 알기가 쉽겠습니까? 예를 들어, 펄펄 끓는 물을 가지고 여러분들한테 이게 펄펄 끓는다고 얘길 해도 그건 여러분한테 말뿐일 테니 참 어려운 일입니다. 여러분이 직접 먹어보든 만져보든 해야 그것이 얼마나 뜨거운지 찬지 아실 텐데 말이죠.

그러니까 우리가 이렇게 법회날이라도 같이 모여 질문하고 서로 토론하는 겁니다. 이렇게라도 해야 구석구석에 계시는 누구라도 알아 듣는 분은 알아 들을 거고, 지금 못 알아 듣는 분은 요 다음에 알아들을 수도 있는 거니까요. 이렇게 해서 이 세상을 조금이라도 간파할 수 있는 자력(自力)이 생기게 되면 얼마나 좋겠습니까? 그럼 질문하실 분 있으면 질문하세요.

fundamental connection. It's this response that's sometimes called "*Bodhisattva*."[8] But this "Bodhisattva" functions according to the needs of the whole, and ordinary people are unable to see the overall picture.

So when you're dealing with all the ordinary, little things of daily life, it's best to let go of your opinions about how they should go, and just unconditionally entrust that situation. Do this, and let go of any stray thoughts of "me" or "I did."

Take it all, whether it's pleasant or unpleasant, going well or not, and entrust it there. Just go forward like this, doing your best to take care of things as they arise. If it seems like you're surrounded by filthy water, or even clean water, don't fall into blame or resentment. Just entrust it all to your foundation. Then it can change into water that's useful to you.

It's not always so easy to grasp the point I'm trying to make. Take the example of a pot of boiling water. Even though I tell you it's hot, at first those are just words; it's difficult to comprehend what "hot" really means. However, after you pour a cup of water, hold the cup, sniff the water, and finally taste it, then you understand.

질문자 1(남): 큰스님 감사합니다. 이렇게 기회를 베풀어 주셔서 대단히 감사합니다. 저는 한마음[6] 과학원에서 공부하고 있습니다. 오늘 제가 말씀 드릴 것은 사람의 출생과 임신에 대한 몇 가지 의학적인 문제들입니다. 고래(古來)로 불가에서는 사람 몸 받기 힘들고 정법(正法) 만나기 힘들고 또 정법 만나서 수행해서 보리과(菩提果)를 얻기 힘들다고 그랬습니다.

그 첫 번째 과제가 사람이 되는 건데, 사실 온전하게 열 달이 돼서 출산하기까지 상당히 많은 위험과 고통과 문제가 뒤따르고 있습니다. 그에 대한 몇 가지를 여쭙겠습니다.

임신이 되고 나면은 임산부의 약 15%에서 자연유산이 일어나는데 그 원인은 태아의 결함인 경우가 60~70%가 되고 산모에 어떤 결함이 있는 경우도 있습니다. 그리고 대부분 태아 결함이

---

6. 한마음: '한'이란 광대무변함, 일체가 하나로 합쳐진 것을 뜻하며, 한마음이란 만질 수도 없고 보이지도 않으며, 시공간을 초월하여, 시작도 끝도 없는 근본마음을 말함. 또한, 만물만생의 마음이 삼천대천 세계와 서로 연결되어 하나로 돌아가는 것을 의미하기도 함. 다시 말해, 한마음은 우주 전체와 그 속에서 살고 있는 일체 생명들이 근본을 통해 서로 연결되어 그 마음들이 하나로 돌아가는 모든 작용을 포함하고 있음.

In order to understand this formless, fundamental essence that we are, we gather here on the first Sunday of every month. As we talk about this, ask questions, and share our experiences, this will help others understand practice and move forward. Some people understand deeply right away, and in others it bubbles and percolates for a while before understanding begins to dawn. In this way, you can develop the ability to truly understand what's going on. Wouldn't that be wonderful? So if you have a question today, please go ahead and ask.

Questioner 1 (male): Thank you for this opportunity! I've heard it said that it's difficult to be born with a human body, to meet the Dharma, and still more difficult to practice and awaken. As an obstetrician, I find myself often thinking about the first of these, and would like to ask you several questions about pregnancy and childbirth.

During the nine months of pregnancy, there can be a lot of problems. First of all, 15% of women experience a miscarriage. In these cases, we believe that something like 60-70% of them

염색체 기형으로 밝혀지고 있는데 그러한 염색체 이상이 왜 일어나는지, 그게 어떠한 의미가 있는지 잘 모르고 있습니다. 물론 치료법은 없고요. 그래서 전체 임산부의 15%가 유산이 되는 건 전체적으로 보면 상당히 많은 숫자인데 이러한 현상이 왜 생기는 건지, 법의 차원에서 어떠한 까닭이 있는 것이며, 그에 대한 치료는 어떻게 해야 되는 건지 먼저 여쭙고 싶습니다.

큰스님: 그럼 그 질문에 대답을 하기 이전에 한마디 하죠. 다른 신도들도 그런 문제를 가지고 많이 옵니다. 그럴 때에 나는 열심히 주인공에다 관(觀)[7]하라고 합니다. 그런데 주인공 자리에 모든 걸 놓되 그냥 있어서는 안돼요. 아기 주인공과 통신을 해야죠. 그러니깐 내가 관하라고 말할 때는 그냥 말로만 한다든지 보이는 것만을 갖고 말하는 게 아니다 라는 얘깁니다.

---

7. 관(觀): 어의적으로 '관찰하다' '보다'라는 뜻을 가지고 있으며, 마음공부를 하는 과정에서는 '참나'인 주인공을 믿고 맡기는 것을 뜻함. 즉, 삶에서 부딪치는 모든 문제들을 주인공만이 해결할 수 있다는 철저한 믿음으로 주인공에게 맡겨 놓고 분별없이 집착 없이 지켜보는 것을 통틀어 '관'이라 함.

are due to birth defects with the baby, and most of these are chromosomal aberrations. We don't know why these happen, and there's nothing we can do to treat them. A certain percentage of miscarriages also occur due to biological issues with the mothers.

That 15% of all women should experience a miscarriage seems like quite a large number to me. If it's possible, could you tell me why these happen? What is the significance of these in terms of the Dharma, and how can I do a better job of treating expectant mothers?

Kun Sunim: Many people have come to me with similar problems. The first thing I tell them is to sincerely rely upon their foundation and entrust it with the problem. However, there's more to it than simply letting go: the parents also have to connect and communicate with the fetus's foundation. This reliance upon our foundation, Juingong, has to be more than just words – it has to be move beyond just what we can see and touch.

Let me give you an example. Even though a fetus has spent its life in its mother's womb, it

예를 들어 알기 쉽게 말씀을 드리겠습니다. 아기가 현재 뱃속에 들어 있어도 현재의 그 몸 안에 과거의 것을 가지고 있단 말입니다. 때론 과거의 어떠한 영향으로 아기가 유산되려고 할 때가 있는데 그럴 때 아기 주인공한테 얘기하세요. '니가 그 아기를 형성시키는 거니까 잘 데리고 나와야 하잖아.'라고 말입니다. 그런 마음이 통하면 대부분 아기가 자기를 수습합니다. 그런데 어찌하다보면 태반이 옆댕이로 기울어지기도 하죠. 그러면 아기가 거북하니깐 그 안에서 몸을 돌리다가 탯줄이 목에 감길 수도 있고, 아니면 입을 막을 수도 있고요. 그럼 위험한 상태가 되기도 하죠. 그러니깐 될 수 있으면 계속 관하라 그러는 겁니다. 거기에 코치가 들어가야만이 수습을 잘할 테니까요.

질문자 1: 감사합니다. 다음 질문 올리겠습니다. 임신 초기에 거의 대부분의 산모들이 입덧을 경험합니다. 사람 따라 경중의 차이는 있는데 어떤 산모들은 입덧을 못 견뎌가지고 수술을 하기도 하거든요. 그런데 이 입덧에 대해서 의학적으로는 아직 뚜렷한 원인이 없고, 물론 대책도 없습니다. 이에 대해서 큰스님의 가르침을 부탁드리겠습니다.

still carries with it all the baggage of its past lives. Sometimes this influence can cause a miscarriage; if a mother feels something like this, she should speak directly to the baby's foundation: "You made this baby, so you should ensure that the child is born healthy." In this way, parents can guide the baby's foundation to help take care of its body.

Let me give you another example. Sometimes the placenta ends up too far down the side of the uterus. In this case, the baby might be uncomfortable enough that it changes position and accidentally wraps the umbilical cord around its neck, or gets it in its mouth. So, it's good to keep relying upon your foundation. The directions you input to your foundation are communicated to the baby's foundation, which then works to take care of the child.

Questioner 1: Thank you. The next thing I'd like to ask you about is morning sickness. Most women experience this to some extent, but for some women, it's quite serious. For some, it's so severe that they choose to have an abortion. We don't know why women have morning sickness,

큰스님: 어려운 게 아닙니다. 임신을 했을 때, 아기의 원소하고 엄마의 원소하고 완전히 결부가 되면 아무 입덧이 없습니다.

모든 게 아주 어려운 것처럼 보이지만 해결방법을 알면 쉽고, 쉽지만 그 방법을 모르면 아주 어려운 거겠죠. 모든 걸 근본자리에 놓고 아기 주인공과 통신을 하면 알아서 해결을 하기 시작합니다. 주인공에 맡기는 방법이 아닌 다른 방법을 얘기 하자면, 입덧을 해결할 수 있는 부위가 모체에 있긴 해요. 척추 중에도 있고 또 머리 정수리에도 있고 왼쪽 다리에도 있죠. 그렇지만 잘못했다가는 말을 못할 수도 있고, 심각한 문제가 더 많이 생깁니다.

질문자 1: 다음 질문 올리겠습니다. 임신이 쭉 진행이 되면 약 11%의 산모들은 열 달을 못 채우고 36주 이전에 조산을 하게 됩니다. 특히 그 중에서 7%는 35주 이전에 조산을 하고 이렇게 태어난 아이들은 약 15% 정도 목숨을 잃게 되는데, 살아남은 아기도 상당히 많은 수가 몇 달 동안 심각한 후유증을 앓게 됩니다. 그리고 그 아이들이 나중에 또 어른이 돼서 아기를 낳을 때, 조산을 하기도 하고 다른 여러 가지 심각한

nor how to truly cure it. Could you please talk about this?

Kun Sunim: That's not a difficult problem. If all the things that make up the fetus and mother– their essence, cells, hormones, and so on – can connect with and accept each other, then there will be no more morning sickness.

Even a problem like this turns out to be easy once you understand how to solve it. When a mother communicates to her baby's foundation what needs to be done, then that will begin working to make it happen. In fact, there are also three places on a mother's body that can be used to treat morning sickness: the top of her head, the spine, and the left leg. But, these are all somewhat dangerous if you don't truly know what you're doing, and can lead to bad side effects, such as the mother being left unable to speak.

Questioner 1: The next question I'd like to ask you is about premature birth. Statistically, 11% of pregnant women give birth before the 36th week of pregnancy, and 7% of women give birth before the 35th week. Of children born before the

문제가 따르는데 이러한 조산을 예방하는 게 정말 중요합니다. 예방책이나 조산을 진정시킬 수 있는 치료법이 있으면 스님께서 가르쳐 주시기 바랍니다.

큰스님: 지금 현대 의학에서 제시할 수 있는 조산 예방법을 말씀하시는 것 같은데 그런 예방법을 하나의 방편으로 쓸 수는 있지만 조산을 100% 막지는 못합니다. 그 방편이 완전하려면, 예를 들어 손이 들어가서 처치를 해야 되는데 그렇게 할 수는 없지 않습니까? 그러기 때문에 아기하고 통신을 하라는 겁니다. 아기한테 통신이 되면 그런 문제가 해결이 될 수가 있죠. 정말입니다.

조산이 되는 이유를 자세히 얘기할 수는 없지만, 많은 경우 모체에 삼 분파로 나누어진 부분이 한데 잘 합쳐져야 되는데 그게 잘 되지 않으면 기울어지게 되고 태반에 손상이 가기 때문입니다. 잘못하면 태반의 절반이 찢어지기도 하고요.

35th week, 15% don't survive, and many of the rest suffer effects that follow them for the rest of their lives.

Another problem seems to also be that women born prematurely are themselves more likely to give birth to premature babies and to have more problems during the birth. Thus, preventing premature birth is quite an important issue. Is there anything we can do to prevent this or to delay the onset of labor?

Kun Sunim: Even if there was some method like that, it wouldn't be fully effective. Just to give you a very limited, simple example, it's almost impossible for doctors to successfully go in with their hands and correct something with the baby, right? This is why I'm always telling parents to work on communicating with the fetus. If they can truly connect with it, then that problem will immediately start dissolving. Truly. There are so many variables that it's not possible for me to go into all of the reasons why a mother might give birth prematurely.

In general though, many times it's because there are three parts of a mother's body that need to be working together harmoniously, but which

질문자 1: 큰스님 말씀대로 조산의 원인 중에 제일 많은 게 태반조기박리라고 태반이 미리 찢어지는 현상이거든요. 그런 현상이 조산의 주요한 원인으로 밝혀져 있습니다.

큰스님: 그러니깐 아기 원소 자체하고 통신이 되면, 아기 모습은 그걸 알아 듣지 못하지만 그 원소는 알아 듣거든요. 자기 과거의 인연과 부모의 인연을 따라서 형성시킨거니 그 모습을 잘 이끌어야지 하는 의지가 있지 않겠어요? 그러니까 자꾸 아기와 통신을 하라고 하는 거에요.

사실 좋은 영가를 얻으려면 어린애 갖기 전부터 관하라고 합니다. 한 달 전부터도 좋고 석 달 전도 좋고요. 하지만 그럴 새 없이 임신이 됐다면 임신이 된 태(胎)에 좋은 생각으로 좋은 말로 교육을 자꾸 하면 됩니다. 건강하고 좋은 모습을 얻기 위해서도 그렇게 해야 하고 여러 가지 다른 것을 위해서이기도 하죠. 태아교육이라는 게 아주 중요합니다. 지금 뱃속에서부터 장애를 갖고 나오는 일이 많지 않습니까?

aren't. If these are out of balance, the placenta will be damaged, and in some cases it will even begin to separate from the uterus.

Questioner 1: As you say, what we call placental abruption, where the placenta partially peels away from the wall of the uterus, is considered to be the most common cause of premature birth.

Kun Sunim: When, through her foundation, a mother communicates with her unborn child, the child's body can't perceive that, but its own essence, its foundation, hears what the mother is saying. That baby is a being who has evolved through millions of years and who has a great desire and ability to grow and improve, so if the parents are aware of a developing problem, it's to this baby and its foundation that they need to be communicating.

Actually, before getting pregnant, you can raise the intention that a good being will be born through you. Raise this intention and entrust it to your foundation. Doing this for a month before conception is fine. Or for three months is also fine.

뭐 얼마 전에 이런 일이 있었습니다. 한 임신한 신도님이 병원에 갔는데 어린애가 엄마 뱃속에서 정상적으로 자라기 힘드니 수술을 해 일찍 아기를 꺼내야 한다고 그러더랍니다. 그런데 그래도 아기가 살 가망이 희박하다고 그러는데 그 아이가 삼대 독자이고 처음 생긴 아이래요.

그 신도님이 생각해 보니까 너무 기가 막힌 거예요. 여러 가지 상황이 지금 아기가 잘못되면 이혼까지 갈 수도 있는, 순탄하게 살기는 힘든 그런 형편이었죠. 그래서 그걸 지켜보다가 생각다 못해 내가 그랬습니다. "의사가 오진을 한 모양이야. 아이는 아무 문제가 없어. 내가 보니까 괜찮으니 걱정하지 말아. 그러고 열심히 관해."

Even if the parents didn't do anything like this before becoming pregnant, the influence of their kind and harmonious thoughts will continue to help the unborn child grow in that direction. Truly. And it even helps in the years after the child is born.

A healthy baby and attractive appearance are only a few of the many benefits of this kind of communication. This is so important and is capable of correcting many of the handicaps a child could be born with.

A while ago a pregnant woman came here in tears. She'd gone to the hospital for a checkup and received terrible news. The doctor said there was a problem with her baby, and that it would have to be delivered early by cesarean section. He added that it was unlikely the baby would survive, nor would she be able to have children again.

You can imagine how devastating this news was. On top of this, it was her first child, and both her husband and father-in-law had been only children. If she were unable to have children, there would have been immense family pressure on her husband to divorce her.

I thought about what I could say to her. She didn't know anything about how to practice, so

아무 것도 모르는 그 사람더러 어떻게 하라고 애기를 해 봤자 소용이 없는 거고 또 내가 그 상황을 안다고 아는 걸 애기하는 것도 소용없는 겁니다. 그 때에는 그 아기만 그대로 건강하게 잘 있으면 되는 거니까 그 아기의 원소 자체, 아기를 있게 한 그 근본과 통신을 한 거죠. 그러고 나서 나중에 아이를 낳았는데 아주 건강하다고 기별이 왔더군요. 그게 의사의 오진이 아니에요.

그런 아기들은 박사님들이 어찌 해 볼 수가 없어요. 그래서 아무리 박사님이 잘 하신다고 해도, 척추 끄트머리 부분의 뭐 어떤 부분을 통해 아기가 정상적으로 잘 클 수 있게 할 수 있다곤 하지만 그게 그렇게 해 가지고 되는 게 아니거든요. 이것은 아기의 차원과도 관계있는 문제니까요.

최선의 해결책은 마음으로 통신하는 수밖에 없습니다. 구정물이 들어왔다고 하더래도 맑은 물로 바꿔 쓰는 거지요. 단순히 이런 문제뿐만 아니라 모든 것을 다 그렇게 해결할 수 있습니다.

that would have been of little use. Nor would there have been any point in telling her the reason for the baby's problems. How could that have helped the child?

So I communicated directly with the baby's foundation, and told it what it needed to do. Then, all that was needed was for it to remain inside its mother. I told her the doctor had misdiagnosed the situation, and that the baby would be fine. I said not to worry, and to start working on entrusting her wishes for the baby's health to her foundation. Some time later, she gave birth to a healthy child. In truth, the doctor hadn't been mistaken in his diagnosis.

There's nothing doctors can do for babies with that condition. While some doctors think it might be possible to cure it by treating the area around the bottom of the baby's spine, this won't work. It will fail because the essence of the problem is related to the baby's level of mind. So, to resolve the problem, the parents should communicate with the baby's foundation.

In this way, even if you encounter some dirty water, you can change it to clean water. This is also how to solve all other problems as well.

질문자 1: 다음 질문 여쭙겠습니다. 산모가 진통을 겪게 되면 약 5%의 경우에서 아기 상태가 나빠집니다.

그 원인들은 여러 가지가 있는데 오늘날 첨단의 태아 감시 장치를 부착시켜서 태아하고 산모를 관찰하면 한 5% 정도의 아기는 여러 가지 나쁜 소견을 보여서 적절한 처치를 하다가 안 되면 제왕절개수술을 해서 아기를 끄집어냅니다.

그런데 그렇게 하더라도 일단 나빠진 아기를 다시 100% 좋게 만들 수는 없습니다. 수술을 하더라도 나중에 후유증 때문에 뇌성마비 같은 장애가 생길 수 있습니다. 그리고 저희가 의사로서 할 수 있는 거는 거기까지입니다. 그래서 분만 진통 중에 나빠진 아기를 마음법으로도 다시 소생시킬 수 있는 좋은 묘책이 있는지 큰스님께 여쭙고 싶습니다.

큰스님: 뱃속에서 나빠진 애들이나 거꾸로 되어 있는 아기들 얘기가 많아요. 거꾸로 되어 있는 아기가 한번 돌아서 바로 서게끔 하는 것도 아기 원소가 다 해야죠. 그래서 태교를 해라, 태교를 해라 하는 거예요. 아기와 통신을 하며 자꾸 관해라 그럽니다.

Questioner 1: My next question is about labor. When labor lasts for a long time, in about 5 percent of cases, it causes serious problems for the baby. In those cases, it's urgent that we deliver the baby immediately.

Even with an emergency cesarean section, the baby will still sometimes suffer neurological or other permanent damage. Once this happens, there's normally very little doctors can do.

So I would like to ask you, is there a way we can use our fundamental mind to help babies like this fully recover?

Kun Sunim: Quite a few mothers come to see me because their baby has developed problems while in the uterus, or because it's positioned with its head facing up. It's the baby's foundation that moves and guides it, so if we can communicate with this essence, then getting the baby turned around will be no problem.

This is why I'm always telling parents to communicate with their child. When they entrust their thoughts to their foundation, those good intentions end up being communicated to and guiding their unborn child.

아기 원소는 자기를 이끌어주니까 아기를 있게 한 근본 에너지라고 해도 과언이 아니죠. 그러니까 그 아기 원소한테 통신이 되면 자기를 잘 나오게 할 수 있어요.

아기가 나올 때 발 뒤꿈치가 자궁벽에 딱 닿으면서 거길 누르고 나오면 좀 수월해요. 그래야 산모도 힘이 생기고 아기도 힘이 나서 순산하게 되는 거거든요. 그런데 발뒤꿈치가 거길 닿아서 누르는 거는 아기가 스스로 그렇게 해야지 억지로 그렇게 하게 할 수는 없는거죠. 하지만 관해서 통신이 되면 스스로 그렇게 돼요.

즉 말하자면, 아기의 원소하고 산모의 원소하고 박사님이 관하는 마음하고 동시에 같이 통신이 되면 아주 아기가 힘이 생기고 절대로 나쁘게 되지를 않죠. 그리고 빨리 순산될 수가 있어요.

This is also one of those things that's best taken care of before it becomes a problem. If the parents communicate with the baby's foundation, then this essence, this fundamental energy, will guide the baby through childbirth and make the delivery fairly easy.

If the baby puts her heels next to the placenta and pushes as she moves down and out, then the delivery will go smoothly. When the mother and the baby work together like this, then things will go well.

However, even if the baby puts its heels next to the placenta, we can't force it to push. But if through our foundation we can communicate with that child, then its foundation will guide its feet and help it to push for herself.

In other words, when the baby's essence communicates with that of its mother and the doctor, it will gain strength and won't be harmed by the delivery. And it will be born smoothly and quickly.

By the way, it's not always bad to pause during the labor and delivery. If the baby's connection with its foundation is weak, this is a good chance to reinforce that, as well as to recover its physical energy.

그리고 더디면 더딘 대로 좋은 점도 있어요. 조금 쉬는 동안에 아기가 자기 근본에 모든 걸 의지하며 그 정신력을 다시 더 강하게 집어 넣을 수도 있으니깐요.

우리는 이 정신력이 아니라면 송장이나 다름없습니다. 그러기 때문에 어떤 때 그걸 모르고 그냥 사는 사람을 보면 뭐 참, 그 사람에 대해 욕심나는 게 하나도 없어요. 이걸 말로 하려니깐 힘 드는군요. 이게 말로 해서 되는 게 아닌데 말이에요.

질문자 1: 감사합니다, 스님. 다음 질문 여쭙겠습니다. 이 분만 진통을 겪으면서 약 15%의 아기들은 엄마 뱃속에서 태변이라고 하는 똥을 싸게 됩니다. 그리고 또 그중에 약 15%정도가 그 똥을 그대로 다 코로, 입으로 마셔 가지고 폐 속으로 박히게 되는 경우가 일어납니다. 그럼 이 아이들은 나와서 호흡을 잘 못하게 되고 심하면 사망하기도 하고요.

Ah, this spiritual strength, this ability to reflect upon our foundation and rely upon it! People lacking this seem like mannequins moving along the street. [Sighs.] This functioning of our inherent essence is just so profound and precious; words fail utterly when trying to convey a sense of this.

Questioner 1: Thank you. Kun Sunim. Next, I would like to ask about something called meconium aspiration syndrome. About 15% of babies are born having already excreted their first feces, which we call meconium. Sometimes this happens because of the pain and stress of delivery, and sometimes more naturally.

Of these babies, roughly another 15% have inhaled the meconium, so that it either blocks their breathing or eventually works its way deep into their lungs, where it causes all kinds of problems. Some babies die because of this, and others experience serious health problems.

As an obstetrician, I, too, had a baby die during delivery because of this. Ever since then, I've made sure to entrust the thought that my deliveries should all happen without these kinds

저도 분만 중에 이렇게 사망한 아기를 경험한 적이 있었는데 그 일이 있고 나서는 늘 관해서 그런지 사망사고를 지금까지 겪지 않고 있습니다.

이처럼 아기가 태변을 뱃속에서 싸게 되면 현재로써는 저희 의사들이 해 줄 수 있는 게 전혀 없습니다. 아기가 나온 뒤에 기도를 청소한다든지 하는 그런 방법들이 있긴 하지만 그렇게 해 줘도 아기가 폐 속에 태변이 박혀 가지고 호흡을 못한다든가 하는 문제를 예방할 수는 없습니다.

그래서 이렇게 태변 흡입을 하는 경우, 관하는 것 외에 다른 처치 방법이 있는지 여쭙고 싶습니다.

큰스님: 우리가 지금 부처님 법을 배우고 있습니다. 부처님 법이라고 하기 이전에 여러분들의 마음법을 배우고 있는 거죠.

마음으로 실생활에서 할 수 있는 방편은 여러 가지에요. 예를 들어 엄마가 잘 관하고 그래서 아기와 소통되면 태교를 한다고 말을 할 수 있죠.

of problems, and from that time until now, there have been no more incidents at my clinic.

When a baby excretes feces while in the womb, there's nothing we doctors can do about it except just wait until the baby is born, and hope we can clear the airway if there's a problem. Even when this works, it still can't prevent the problems that result from having meconium deep in the lungs.

I would like to know if there is anything a doctor can do to treat this, besides just entrusting positive intentions to their foundation?

Kun Sunim: What we are learning here is the truth the Buddha taught about how the world works. Actually, I can say we are learning the truth of how our minds work. And one of the things you will realize is that through this fundamental mind of ours, there are so many different skillful ways we can approach any particular situation. By entrusting the situation to our fundamental mind we can find a path that will work out.

When the parents raise a positive intention and entrust it, it is communicated to the fetus.

그리고 이런 식의 태교를 하게 되면 아기가 엄마 뱃속에서 자라서 나올 때까지 조금도 위험한 압박을 받지 않아요. 그거를 박사님들은 진정으로 믿고 아셔야 돼요.

그런데 그러질 못하면 아기가 마음이 급해져서 허겁지겁 몸을 둥글리게 되고, 경우에 따라 태변을 싸게 되는 거죠. 그러면 나오면서 선생님이 말씀한 대로 문제가 생길 수 있는 거에요. 어찌됐건 나와야 되는데 몸을 둥글린다는 건 문제가 왔다는 얘기니까 그렇게 되지 않게 지속적으로 관해 줘야죠.

옛날에는 산모 머리 위에다 참기름을 세 번 칠해주었다는데 그러면 아기가 아무런 손상이 없이 나온다는 말이 있었어요. 그게 우스운 방편 같지만, 내 생각에는 세 번 머리에 찍어주는 것이 삼세심이 잘 돌아가 순산하라는 사람들의 마음이 담겨 있는 게 아닌가 여겨집니다.

질문자 1: 스님, 산모 머리의 어느 쪽에 찍어주는 겁니까? 앞쪽인가요? 뒤쪽인가요?

We call this *taegyo*, or prenatal education. If parents can guide and comfort the baby like this, it won't experience any dangerous situations at all. Doctors truly need to understand this, and the possibilities it offers.

If the parents aren't practiced at communicating with the unborn child, then if that baby feels threatened, he or she will try to curl up more tightly. And this can cause them to excrete feces, which leads to other problems. Of course, if they're curled up at the time of delivery, that's a serious problem all on its own. So, we need to focus on raising and entrusting the thought that this shouldn't happen and that the baby should be comfortable.

In the old days, midwives with these intentions for the baby put three dabs of sesame oil on the mother's head. It seems a bit silly to us now, but it contained their sincere hopes for a smooth delivery and a healthy child.

Questioner 1: Where on the head should the sesame oil be placed? In the back, or in the front?

큰스님: 박사님 마음대로 하세요. 아마 정수리겠죠. 중요한 건 이 원소 자체는 수천 년 전 과거에도 있었고 또 미래에도 있을 거고 현재에도 있으니까 이거야말로 보배 아닌 보배라는 겁니다. 아기든지 어른이든지 우리 모두 이끌어 가는 선장이 있지 않습니까? 이 선장은 모두를 잘 이끌려 하는 마음이 있기 때문에 선장한테 모든 것을 믿고 맡긴다면 절대로 잘못되지 않습니다.

질문자 1: 마지막 질문 여쭙겠습니다. 분만을 다 마치고 나면 대단히 불행하게도 상당히 많은 수의 산모들이 하혈을 하게 됩니다. 대부분의 산모들은 자궁수축제를 투여하게 되면 출혈이 멎고 별 탈이 없는데 그 중에는 하혈이 멎지 않아서 자궁 적출술을 받는다든지 혹은 생명을 잃는 경우가 지금도 적지 않습니다. 그래서 저처럼 마음공부[8]가 덜 되어 있는 산부인과 의사들은 이런 어려운 분만이나 산모를 굉장히 두려워합니다.

---

8. 마음공부: 진정한 자유인이 되기 위해 자신의 마음이 어떻게 작용하고 변하는지를 관찰하고 배우며, 그것을 실제 생활 속에서 응용하고 체험해 보면서 알아가는 모든 과정을 뜻함.

Kun Sunim: Wherever you like. Just on the top of the head. The important thing is this essence, this foundation. That's always been with us. It's a treasure beyond treasure that has existed throughout all time. Every single one of us has this captain, no matter whether we're grown adults or unborn children. This captain is ever trying to guide us in positive directions, so if we just entrust it with whatever arises, it will never, ever lead us astray.

Questioner 1: This is my final question. Unfortunately, there are quite a few women who suffer from excessive bleeding following the delivery. Most women respond to injections of a drug type known as a uterotonic, which works to stop the bleeding, but some do not.

In those cases, surgically removing the uterus is the only option left, but some women still die before this can happen, or during the surgery. This problem in particular scares obstetricians.

These problems I've asked about today are ones that the medical field is unable to completely resolve. The longer a doctor in my field works, the more likely he or she is to encounter one of these

지금까지 제가 말씀드린 여러 가지 문제가 아직까지는 의학의 힘으로 완전히 해결할 수 없는 거고 언제 이런 환자가 닥칠지 아무도 예측을 못하기 때문에 산부인과를 하면 할수록 더욱 더 두려움과 공포심을 갖게 됩니다.

그리고 지금 말씀드린 이 마지막 문제가 사실 제일 심각합니다. 산후에 출혈하는 거는 예측도 불가능하고, 워낙 급작스럽게 일어나는데다 출혈이 꼭 수도꼭지로 물 틀 때처럼 펑펑 나옵니다. 그러니까 일이십 분 동안 급하게 혈압이 떨어지기도 하고, 아주 좋지 않은 경우가 많습니다.

이런 경우에 저는 관하는 도리를 많이 활용을 하고 있습니다만, 큰스님께서 달리 알려주실 방편이 있으시면 말씀해 주시기 바랍니다.

큰스님: 지금 말씀 드리는 것은 방편이 아니고 실제입니다. 주인공은 이름이고 주인공에게 맡긴다는 것도 방편이지만 실질적으로는 내가 관한다 안 한다 할 게 아닙니다. 자연스럽게 그대로 인식이 돼야 된다는 이야깁니다.

emergencies, and the more worried they become that a patient will have one of these problems.

Of these, bleeding is the worst, and completely unpredictable. It happens very suddenly, and the blood flows like tap water. The woman's blood pressure will continue to drop sharply, and over the next ten or twenty minutes, many very, very bad things will occur.

In cases like this, I rely very heavily upon what you've taught us about raising one thought and entrusting it to our foundation. Is there anything else I should be doing? I'd be grateful for anything you could share with me.

Kun Sunim: What I've taught you isn't merely some technique, but how things actually work. Of course, "Juingong" and "foundation" are labels, and "entrust it to your foundation" is also a method, but they work towards the same, one thing: clearing the way, or opening the channel, so to speak, so that your foundation can recognize what's going on. Then, if something serious begins to appear, your foundation is able to immediately perceive it and so can respond right away.

예를 들어 하혈을 하는 건 위험하니깐 아예 그렇게 되지 않게 해야 한다는 것을, 근본에서 그걸 인식해야 한다는 얘깁니다. 근본과 하나 되어 그렇게 되지 않게끔 하라고 단정 지어 결정을 하면 그렇게 되는 겁니다.

자기 공체(共體)에 들어 있는 자기 원소가 진짜 자기라는 걸 믿고 알아야 합니다. 그런데 박사님이 만약, 잠시라도 딴 생각을 하면서 딴 데로 빠지면 근본에 100% 일임을 하는 게 아니죠. 내가 신임을 완전히 하지 않는 이상 거기도 내 말을 믿지 않고 듣지 않아요.

옛날에 공부를 하다가 내면의 나에게 "넌 어디서 왔니?" 하고 물어보니까, "일어나서 거울을 봐." 이러는 겁니다. 그래서 거울을 보니 내 얼굴이 보이는 게 아닙니까? 그러자 다시 내면의 내가 "그 얼굴을 보니깐 똑같지?" 그래요. 그래서 "똑같은데." 그랬더니 "이렇게 겉모습은 똑같지만 내가 너라고 할 수도 없고 나라고 할 수도 없다. 보이지 않는 정신계에서는 내가 수없이 바뀐다. 화(化)해서 바뀌니까 보이는 너는 거기에 발끝도 못 쫓아온다. 그러니 그 뜻을 알아라." 하는 겁니다.

If you are openly connected with your foundation like this, then even before the surgery, if you raise the firm determination that nothing should go wrong, then this manifests into reality.

However, this comes with one condition: you have to truly know and believe that the essence that does this is also what you truly are. You are nothing else. That which can respond fully and completely is your true nature, your true essence: that which you are now and have always been. If you miss this point, it will be difficult to completely believe in this essence. If you don't have confidence in what you truly are, how can you, as your true nature, respond confidently and completely?

A long time ago, I asked my inner self, "Where did you come from?"

It answered, "Stand up and look in a mirror." So I got up and looked in a mirror.

"The face in the mirror looks just like your face, doesn't it?"

"Yes," I replied.

My inner self continued, "Even though we have the same face, you can't say that that appearance is me, nor can I say that I am you, because in the unseen realm, I am ceaselessly

모든 사람은 정말 훌륭한 묘법을 가지고 있는데도 그걸 써먹지 못하는 것은 이 모습 가진 내가 전부인 줄 알고 살기 때문입니다.

예전에도 그런 얘기 한 번 했죠. 모습 가진 나는 자(子)가 되고, 바로 보이지 않는 자기는 부(父)가 된다고요. 산으로 다닐 때 묘지가 나란히 두 개 있는 데서 잠시 쉬려는데, 하나는 아비 묘이고 하나는 자식 묘라는 말이 떠오르더니 '부(父)가 자(子)로 오면 자(子)로 하나가 되고, 자(子)가 부(父)로 가면 부(父)로 하나가 되는데 그건 무슨 연고로 그렇게 되느냐?' 하는 겁니다.

그건 내가 날 가르치는 거였겠죠. 그런데 그 말을 가만히 생각해 보니 그 부가 내 모습으로만 있는 게 아니라 쓸모 있게 이걸 화해서 변경을 해야 되겠다고 하면 그냥 그대로 바뀌는 거더라고요. 이게 실제 벌어지는 일인 거죠. 그러니까 이건 말로 어떻게 표현할 수 없을 만큼 희한하지만 실제 나타나는 일이기 때문에 선지식들은 "참 묘하다. 그건 도깨비 장난 같구나."라고 말하기도 했어요.

changing and taking different forms. I continuously change and manifest, and the power of this is vastly beyond anything you can imagine. Discover for yourself what this truly means!"

All people have this supreme ability, but they can't use it because they think that this material self is all they are.

To put it another way, it's like the self with the physical body is the son, and the unseen self is the father. A long time ago, when I lived in the mountains, I stopped to rest next to two graves.[9] As I was leaning against one of them, I heard a voice within me say, "One grave belongs to a father, and the other to his son. If the father visits the son, both become the son; if the son visits the father, both become the father. Why is this?"

This was me teaching myself. That is to say, it was my true self teaching my present consciousness. As I reflected upon this question, the meaning became clear: the father doesn't just sit there with one shape. It manifests and takes whatever shape would be helpful. It automatically takes whatever form is needed.

---

9. In Korea, traditional graves are formed with a rounded mound of dirt and grass, about a meter high.

그러니깐 만약에 박사님이 진짜로 박사님의 원소 자체, 주인공을 믿는다면 그런 걱정은 하나도 할 게 없어요. 주인공한테 '문제가 생기면 안 되니까 끝까지 잘 이끌어야 해.' 하고 관하세요.

옛날에 이런 일도 있었습니다. 어떤 가족이 찾아와 산모가 위험하니 병원으로 같이 가 상황을 봐 달라고 간절히 요청했습니다. 병원에 가보니 아기를 낳고 하혈을 했는데 피가 코로도 나오고 이마 안쪽으로도 출혈이 있어서 다 죽게 돼 호흡기 꽂고 간신히 버티고 있었습니다. 그런데 내가 뭐라고 그런 줄 아세요? 그 가족들에게 산모를 내일 퇴원시키겠느냐고 물었어요.

그 소리를 의사들이 들었다면 미쳤다고 그러지 그거 제정신이라고 그랬겠어요? 그런데 그 가족들이 조금의 망설임도 없이 산모를 퇴원시키겠다고 하는 거예요. 그 말을 듣고 나는 그 병원에서 나왔는데 5분쯤 지나서 피가 다 멎은 거예요.

Words just can't describe this. It is so strange and mysterious, yet it's truly happening all around us in our lives. This is why awakened people of old sometimes said that it was as if the *Dokkaebi*[10] were playing games with us.

If you have strong faith that your essence is working like this, there will be nothing to worry about. Just raise the thought, "There should be no problems with the delivery. From beginning to end, the entire process should go smoothly!" Make this a firm decision!

Years ago I was visited by the family of a woman who had suffered severe complications during childbirth. They begged me to visit her in the hospital, saying her condition was critical. So, I went to the hospital with them. It seemed that after giving birth, the woman had bled excessively; even blood vessels in her sinuses had burst and were still bleeding. The doctors had put her on a respirator, and were just barely able to keep her alive.

---

10. Dokkaebi: A type of sprite or fairy from Korean folklore. In appearance they resemble ogres, and have wooden clubs that have the magical power to create things. They sometimes play tricks on bad people, but will also reward and help good people.

이런 걸 말로 어떻게 합니까? 말로 설명할 수 있는 게 아닙니다. 주인공, 자기 근본마음의 작용으로 어디가 어떻게 되고 어디가 어떻게 됐다는 거를 다 알아도 그건 말로 설명할 수가 없는 겁니다. 박사님 한 찰나의 한 생각이 그렇게 할 수 있는 것입니다.

질문자 1: 스님, 장시간 대단히 감사합니다.

큰스님: 이 주인공이라는 에너지가, 우리가 자꾸 공부를 하게 되면 그 에너지가 그게 에너지 주장자(柱杖子)[9]가 되죠.

질문자 2(남): 스님 감사합니다. 저는 한마음과학원 의학분과에서 공부하고 있습니다. 제가 위내시경 검사를 하면서 경험한 것을 말씀드리고 질문 올리겠습니다.

---

9. 주장자(柱杖子): 일반적으로 선사(禪師, 스님)들이 좌선할 때나 설법할 때 들고 다니는 지팡이를 말함. 행을 통해 흔들리지 않는 마음의 중심이 서게 되는 것을 뜻함. 마음공부 과정에서는 안팎에서 일어나는 모든 문제를 내면의 근본마음 한 곳에 맡겨 놓는, 참선수행을 통해 흔들리지 않는 마음의 중심이 서게 되는 것을 말함.

I entrusted the situation inwardly, and can you guess the words that arose from within me? "Will you have her released from the hospital tomorrow?" If the doctors had heard that, they would have thought I was crazy!

However, the family never hesitated and said they would. Hearing their answer, I left the hospital. Five minutes later, the bleeding stopped!

Words just can't explain this. It's something beyond them. Even though I completely understand how these things happen through the functioning of our foundation, words just can't encompass them.

Yet a single thought, raised well and entrusted to your foundation, can function like this.

Questioner 1: Thank you for such detailed answers.

Kun Sunim: This energy of our foundation…. The more we practice relying on our foundation, the more this energy becomes a great pillar that supports our life.

저는 위내시경 검사를 할 때에 항상 관하고 합니다. '주인공 당신이 하는 거지. 나는 심부름만 할 테니 환자가 편안하게 해야지.' 하고 관하고 검사를 합니다.

며칠 전에 구역질이 잘 나는 환자에게 위내시경 검사를 한 적이 있었는데 검사하기 전에 항상 하듯이 또 관했습니다. 그런데 이번에는 좀 더 깊이 관해지며 제가 뒤로 쑥 빠지며 간절해지는 걸 느끼게 됐고, 순간 내 마음이 환자와 통함을 느꼈습니다. 그 순간부터 환자는 편안하게 내시경 검사를 받았습니다.

이 체험을 바탕으로 감기환자나 위장병환자를 진료할 때에 또 그렇게 관하려 했으나 그렇게 되지를 않았습니다. 그래서 '환자가 잘 낫기를' 하고 마음만 내었습니다. 질문 올리겠습니다.

환자를 진료할 때에 마음이 모아져서 좀 더 깊이 관해지면서 제가 쑥 뒤로 빠지며 근본과 통하는 거와 환자가 잘 낫기를 바라는 마음만 내는 것과는 어떠한 차이가 있습니까?

Questioner 2 (male): Thank you, Kun Sunim. I am a doctor, and perform many endoscopies. First, I'd like to tell you about an experience I had, and then I'll ask my question. Whenever I perform an endoscopy, I raise a thought for the patient like this, "Juingong, you're the one doing this, and the one who can make the patient comfortable. I'm just running errands in the material realm." Then I entrust this thought to my foundation.

A few days ago, before I performed an endoscopy on a patient who easily becomes nauseated, I raised a thought like this and sincerely entrusted it to my foundation. This time, "I" seemed to disappear, and the patient and I were one. From the very start, the patient had no discomfort during the procedure.

Later, I tried the same thing with other patients who had colds and digestive issues, but I couldn't feel anything, so I just raised a thought for their quick recovery. My question is this: What is the difference between those times when my mind becomes very sincere, where my sense of "me" fades away and I truly feel a connection with my patients, and those times when this feeling is completely missing?

다시 말씀드리자면, 환자를 진료할 때에 마음이 간절하게 모아져서 제가 뒤로 쏙 빠지면서 마음 근본과 통하는 걸 느낄 때가 있습니다. 그런 경우는 자주 있지는 않고 제가 급하거나 마음이 바삐 돌아갈 때 그리 되는 경우가 있습니다. 그런데 보통 진료실에서 환자를 볼 때는 그렇게 순간적으로 몰입이 되지 않아 그냥 환자가 잘 나았으면 하고 마음을 냅니다.

큰스님: 박사님이 간절하게 마음을 내서 그렇게 통하는 걸 자꾸 경험해 그렇게 된다는 걸 안다면 진짜로 믿어지시죠?

질문자 2: 예.

큰스님: 완전히 믿어지면 박사님이 그냥 그렇게 생각만 해도 환자의 인체에 박사님을 포함한 전체 에너지가 들어가게 되는 겁니다.

박사님이 그냥 낸 생각이 그렇게 된다는 뜻이 아니라 근본과 하나가 되어 나오는 생각이어야만이 자유롭게 화해서 인체에 들어갈 수 있다는 겁니다. 그래서 박사님이 들어가게 되는 겁니다. 박사님 자신은 그걸 모르시지만 말입니다.

Both times, I think I'm being equally sincere, but the first case doesn't happen very often. I wonder if I'm not actually as sincere most times, due to the lack of urgency in the patient's situation.

Kun Sunim: Once you've had those experiences of sincerely entrusting a thought and then feeling that sense of connection with your patients, you gain deeper faith in your foundation and how it works, right?

Questioner 2: Yes.

Kun Sunim: When your faith that you are already one with your foundation becomes very firm and grounded, then with just the thought that the procedure needs to go well, your energy and the energy of the whole enters the patient and works towards that outcome.

I don't mean to say that this will happen with ordinary or random thoughts. It has to be a thought entrusted so thoroughly that it becomes one with your foundation. Then it can become something that manifests into the world. Then it will function in many different ways, which you

어떤 경우에는 박사님이 열 명, 스무 명으로 화하기도 합니다.

예를 들어 만약 환자의 인체에 막힌 부분이 있어 떼내야만 하는데, 수술을 할 수 없는 경우라든지, 백혈병 같은 질병으로 에너지가 나오지 않는다든가 하는 문제가 있으면 박사님이 환자 안으로 들어가 일을 해야 합니다. 그 자기 하나가 화해서 의사 서너 명이 되어 보이지 않는 수술을 해야 합니다. 그리고 그렇게 보이지 않는 데서 수술을 하고 나도 그건 찰나입니다.

지금 말씀드린 것을 박사님이 대략 아시는 대로 자꾸 하시다 보면 나중에는 보이지 않는 데서 어떻게 돌아가는지 아시게 되겠죠. 그거를 도(道)라고 하죠. 굳이 도란 말을 붙이지 않더라도 박사님이 진짜 그렇게 할 줄 아셔야 되겠죠.

그러니까 평소에 진찰하면서 마음이 급하지 않을 때 '잘 되라.'고 마음 내는 것과 달리 이런 경우에는 '그냥 잘 돼야 돼!'하는 거죠. 그 결정이죠.

may not recognize. Sometimes it may manifest as ten or twenty doctors, working unseen to take care of the patient.

For example, suppose some part of a patient's body is failing, and surgery isn't possible, or they have some disease like leukemia where the body isn't producing enough energy. Then, through this foundation of ours, you have to enter the patient and fix the problem. In this way, you can manifest as multiple unseen doctors who go in and perform surgery. Performing surgery like this, through the unseen realm, takes just an instant.

If you keep practicing, doing the best you can with what you understand, the day will come when you truly understand the wondrous functioning that takes place when you become one with your true essence. This is sometimes called "awakening," or "attaining the way."

Regardless of the labels, this functioning of your true essence is something you need to understand and be able to apply. When you see your ordinary patients, go ahead and entrust their well-being to your foundation. However, when their situation is quite serious, you need to make a firm decision that they will turn out well. This needs to be a decision!

질문자 2: 예, 스님.

큰스님: 그게 결정력입니다. 박사님들이 어떠한 한 가지 문제를 해결하기 위해서가 아니라 자기가 늘 지니고 있어야 하는 보배이기 때문에 자기가 그 자체여야 되지요.

자신은 보이지 않는 자기가 화해서 바뀌는 걸 모르겠지만 그렇게 화해서 바뀌기 때문에 인체로 들어갈 수 있는 겁니다.

예를 들어, 보이지 않는 자기가 환자의 인체로 들어가 수술을 하고 난 뒤라도 환자의 상태가 위험할 경우, 보이지 않는 박사님 모습 하나가 거기 지키고 있어도 무방하게끔 되어 있거든요. 그럴 때는 박사님이 좁쌀 알갱이만하게 돼서 들어가겠죠. 하하 아니, 좁쌀 알갱이도 아니고 흔적 없이, 들어가는 사이 없이 들어가겠죠. 그래서 그것이 묘법이라고 그러는 겁니다.

그러니깐 걱정할 일도 없고, 내가 한다 안 한다 말로 떠벌일 것도 없습니다. 그렇게 할 수 있는 거는 박사님의 마음이 이미 근본과 하나가 되면 그렇게 된다는 거죠. 그렇게 자꾸 실험을 해 보세요. 진짭니다.

Questioner 2: Okay, I understand, Kun Sunim.

Kun Sunim: It's the ability to determine the direction things go. This is a great treasure that you have the potential to attain, and which you need to attain. It's something you need to practice applying across your daily life. You have to keep practicing with this until you utterly become this ability, and can use it instantly, wherever it's needed.

Even though you don't perceive it, your unseen self can transform into anything that's needed, whether seen or unseen. Through this ability it can enter the patient and treat whatever is wrong. If, after this unseen surgery, the patient's condition is unstable, your unseen self can leave behind an invisible doctor to monitor the patient and take care of them until they are okay. When your unseen self enters the patient, its form is vastly smaller than even the tiniest grain of millet, and it enters the patient without leaving any trace behind. This functioning is sometimes called the "Profound Manifestation of the Dharma."

질문자 2: 예. 스님, 열심히 정진하겠습니다.

질문자 3(남): 큰스님 감사합니다. 이렇게 질문을 드리게 돼서 무한한 영광으로 생각합니다. 저는 부산지원 법형제회에서 공부하고 있습니다. 스님의 법문에서 제가 평소에 궁금해 했던 것의 답을 조금 전에 다 들었습니다. 그래도 이왕 나온 김에 질문 두 가지만 드리겠습니다.

첫째 질문은 요즘 흉악범들이 사회를 혼란시키고 도망 다니는 것을 보면 보통 사람들은 언뜻 '저놈 빨리 잡혀야 할 텐데.' 하고 생각합니다. 그렇지만 우리 공부하는 사람은 좀 다르게 마음을 내어야 한다고 생각합니다. 나쁜 짓을 저지르는 범죄자들에게 우리가 어떻게 마음을 내어야 하는지 큰스님의 가르침을 바랍니다.

Thus, there's nothing to worry about, nor any need to talk about what you've done. When you've become one with your foundation, you just do whatever's needed. So, work hard at trying to do this, then you can experience for yourself what I've talked about.

Questioner 2: Thank you. I will work hard at this.

Questioner 3 (male): Thank you, Kun Sunim. I'm deeply grateful for this opportunity to ask you a question. Oddly enough, you just answered the questions I came here with. I'm here though, so I'd like to ask you about two things that have been nagging me.

First, there have been several rather brutal crimes lately, which have caused a lot of commotion. To the extent that most people think about these, they feel that the cops should grab those guys and throw them away in a dark hole somewhere. However, as people who practice, it seems like we need to do more in how we raise thoughts for people who are behaving badly. So, what kinds of thoughts should I be giving rise to?

큰스님: 옛날에 어떤 도둑이 큰 배를 타고 가다가 그 안에서 도둑질을 했습니다. 그리고는 그 배에 계속 타고 있으면 붙잡힐 것 같아서 다른 배로 옮겨 탔어요.

그런데 마침 한 선지식이 그 큰 배에 타고 있었는데, 도둑이 물건 훔친 걸 다 알고 그 사람의 내력을 살펴 보았습니다. 그리고 그 도둑이 아주 비참하게 살아왔고 그러다 보니 도둑질을 해 왔다는 것을 알게 됐습니다.

본인이 하는 짓이 나중에 어떤 결과를 가져 오는지 알면 도둑질을 안 했을 텐데, 모르고 그렇게 계속 살다 보니 그게 습(習)[10]이 돼 인과의 굴레에서 벗어나질 못하고 고생을 하더랍니다.

기본적으로 사람을 해치고자 하는 악한 마음은 없는데 조상이든 인연이든 하여튼 여러 가지 복합적인 이유로 그렇게 도둑질을 하며 살았는데 어찌나 재주가 용한지 그 도둑이 한 번도 붙들려 본 적이 없었습니다.

---

10. 습(習): 현재뿐만 아니라 과거 수 억겁 년 동안 행하였던 모든 행위들(말, 행동, 생각 등)이 버릇이 되어 잠재여력으로 남아 있는 것을 말함.

Kun Sunim: Okay, pay attention. There was a thief who would ride large ships and steal things while they sailed. He never stayed on one ship very long, and would move to a different ship before anyone could catch him.

At last, he stole things from a ship that was also carrying an awakened person. As the thief escaped on a smaller boat, the awakened person perceived what had happened. The awakened one took a careful look into the thief's past, and saw that the thief had grown up in very poor and miserable circumstances, and saw too how his actions were leading him into only more suffering. If the thief had seen this for himself, he would have never stolen a thing.

Unaware of this, he kept stealing. It became a habit, and he became entrapped in the cycle of cause and effect that arose from his actions. Of course, the deeper into this cycle he fell, the more he suffered. The thief wasn't a bad person, and didn't have a desire to harm others; he had just fallen into stealing through a series of complicated events and karmic affinities. The funny thing was, he had never been caught, not even once.

선지식이 그 모든 것을 보시고 그 자리에서 그 도둑이 앞으로는 도둑질을 하지 않도록 도둑질 하는 의식이 조금 붙은 거를 떼어 버렸답니다.

도둑질을 하는 사람이 왜 도둑질을 하게 됐는지를 알고 보면 불쌍하기가 한량없거든요. 그러니까 여러분도 그런 사람들을 나쁘다고만 하지 마시고 이런 저런 걸 잘 헤아려 보세요. 배가 고파서, 식구들을 다 굶겨 죽일 수가 없어서 도둑질을 했다면 붙잡아서 감옥에 보내지 않고도 더 이상 도둑질 하지 않게 할 수 있어요. 그러니깐 따지고 보면 그런 사람은 도둑이라고 해도 도둑이 아니죠.

현실 법에 의하면, 빵 하나를 훔쳐도 도둑이라서 감옥에 가두지마는, 이 부처님 법은 그렇게 훔쳤다 해도 그 원인을 먼저 잘 살펴보고 모두를 다 건지는 겁니다.

The awakened person saw all of that, and perceived that the consciousnesses urging the man to steal were relatively small and overshadowed by his general decency. The awakened person was able to remove those consciousnesses, which then caused the man to lose his desire to steal.

If you had seen all the reasons why he was stealing, you, too, would have felt such deep pity and sympathy for him. So, don't just reflexively criticize those who are behaving badly. Instead, try to understand where their behavior is coming from. If someone is hungry, if their family is starving, and stealing was the only way he could support them, then sending him to jail may not be the best option. There are other ways to keep him from stealing. Even though people like this are called thieves, they are not thieves in the true meaning of the word.

According to the law, someone who steals even a loaf of bread is a thief, and can be jailed. However, if we follow the spirit of the Buddha's teachings, we need to look into the causes underlying the theft, and then work to save everyone involved.

예를 들어, 도둑질하는 의식 때문에 도둑질을 했다면 그 의식을 떼어서 좋은 의식으로 바꿔줘서 좋은 사람으로 살게 하고, 사는 것이 힘들어 도둑질을 했다면 앞으로는 도둑질 안 하고 노력을 해서 살게 만들어 주는 거죠.

부처님 법에서는 '너는 나쁘니깐 유치장으로 가고 너는 좋으니깐 좋은 데로 가거라.' 하는 게 아닙니다. 유치장으로 갈 사람도 유치장으로 안 가게 할 수 있는 것이 보살의 응신이요, 또 지금 옳은 길을 잘 가고 있는 사람은 끝끝내 그렇게 잘 가게끔 하는 것이 부처님의 응신입니다.

그러기 위해 나쁘다 좋다를 떠나라고 하는 겁니다. 나쁘다 좋다를 떠나야 내 마음이 자유스러워지고 그래야 자유자재할 수 있는 거니까요.

그걸 뭐라고 그럴까요? 귀신 방귀 에너지라고 그럴까요? 이렇게 해서 우리들이 우리들을 고르게 다 건질 수 있습니다. 조건 없이 모두를 건진다는 말입니다. 남을 조금도 해롭게 하는 법이 없이 말이죠.

For example, if someone stole due to the actions of underlying states of consciousness, then if we can turn those around, they'll naturally become a good person. Or, if they stole because they're poor and hungry, we can help them earn a living on their own.

"You're a bad person, and must be punished. You're a good person, and so will be sent to a good place." This is not what the Buddha taught! The essence of the word "Bodhisattva" means working to help those destined for jail to instead find a positive path, and helping those who are going in the right direction to keep going in that direction to the very end.

It's so you can do this, that I've told you to let go of judgments of good and bad. When we let go of both "good" and "bad," our minds become free – only then can we attain the freedom to manifest as needed.

What does this mean? Well, what if I called it the energy of a ghost's fart? [Smiles] If you can realize this, then we can save everyone. We can save everyone, unconditionally. And while doing this, we won't harm others in the slightest.

어느 날 화엄경을 잠깐 보았는데 이런 내용이 있었습니다. "부처님 옆으로 지나 가다가 보기만 해도 그 은혜가 말도 못하고, 손만 만져도 그 은혜가 말도 못하고, 얼굴만 쳐다보기만 해도 자기의 죄명이 다 소멸된다."는 거였어요.

얼마나 남을 원망 안하고, 남을 미워 안하고 남에게 나쁜 말을 안 해야 그런 사람이 되겠습니까? "너희들 내 소리, 이 법을 거짓으로 알지 말아라. 진정 너희들이 이 법을 안다면 너희가 진정코 보살이 될 것이니라." 이렇게 말씀하셨거든요.

생각해 보면, 먹기 위해서 하는 일인데 하다보니 언짢은 일이 전부 생깁니다. 서로 죽이고 살리고 하는 싸움박질도 먹고 사는 게 아니라면 왜 생기겠습니까?

언젠가 벌레들이 먹을 것을 뺏기 위해 싸우는 것을 지켜본 적이 있었는데 그 벌레들은 싸우다가도 자기 몸이 싸움을 견디지 못할 것 같으면 먹을 거를 그냥 두고 떠납디다. 돌아서서 떠나더라고요.

Once when I was reading the *Flower Garland Sutra*, I saw the following line. "Just walking by a Buddha results in great blessings. To hold the hand of a Buddha produces unimaginable blessings, and to look a Buddha in the face will lead to the dissolving of all the roots of evil behavior."

Can you imagine how diligently we have to work at not resenting others, at not hating them, and at not saying harsh words, in order to become a person whose presence can be such a blessing? The sutra continued, saying, "This is true, and not false – if you awaken to the truth underlying this, you will become a true Bodhisattva."

Think about this: all kinds of unpleasant things happen in order for us, or any other being, to eat, don't they? Think about all the desperate fighting that surrounds us just for the sake of eating and living.

Long ago, I was watching two bugs fight over a piece of food. Finally one of them couldn't sustain the fight any longer, and abandoned the food. It just turned around and left. I guess that humans, too, should walk away when it doesn't look like they're going to get the prize. Instead,

사람도 자기가 먹지 못할 거라면 벌레처럼 그냥 떠나면 되는데 어떤 사람들은 그거를 악착같이 빼앗아 먹으려고 싸우다 보니 서로 심하게 다치기도 하고 죽기도 하는 거죠. 그런 문제가 우리가 살아 나가는데 결정적으로 작용할 수도 있는 거예요.

그러니깐 누가 뭘 훔치고 달아났다면 '그놈 빨리 붙잡혀야 할 텐데.' 하고 마음 내지 마시고 '이건 어차피 벌어진 일이니까 이번만 붙잡히지 말고 앞으로는 도둑질하지 말고 살아라. 그저 어떡하든지 굶지 말고 잘 살아라.' 이렇게 진심으로 마음을 내 주세요. 그러면 나도 나쁜 마음을 내지 않으니 좋고 상대방도 좋아지니 좋고 서로 다 좋은 겁니다.

질문자 3: 감사합니다. 두 번째 개인적인 일을 질문드리겠습니다. 저는 몇 년 전 조그만 사업을 시작했습니다. 시작하면서 '내가 하는 것이 아니야. 주인공 자리에서 하는 거야.' 하면서 항상 관하면서 함이 없이 한다고 했지만 사업이 잘 안 되어 얼마 전 그만두었습니다.

some people keep struggling and sweating until their bodies are sick and broken. From then on, nothing in their lives is ever the same again.

So, if someone steals something and runs away, don't think, "I hope he gets arrested soon!" Instead, entrust the thought that, "Well, you've already stolen, so this time, don't get caught, but stop stealing. Going forward, live an honest life. Live a life free of fear and poverty." When you raise positive thoughts like this, it's good for the other person, and good for you as well.

Questioner 3: Thank you. My second question is about my own circumstances. A few years ago, I started a small business. From the beginning, I raised the following thought, "I'm not the one doing this; it's my foundation that's running the business." And I made a point of letting go of the thought that "I" was doing things. But things didn't go well, and it wasn't long before I had to close the business.

I made sure to remind myself not to blame others, and in order to pay off my remaining debts, I put another building I owned up for sale. Unfortunately, it still hasn't sold, and as time

절망스러웠지만 그만두면서도 '절대 남을 탓하지 말아야 해. 모든 것은 내 탓이야.' 하고 관했습니다. 그런데 빚을 정리하려고 제가 가지고 있는 건물을 팔려고 내 놓았지만 그것도 잘 팔리지 않고 시시각각으로 갚아야 할 빚만 늘어나고 있습니다.

'오직 주인공만이 해결할 수 있어.' 하고 관하는데도 얼마 안 있으면 빚에 대한 걱정이 슬며시 들고 일어납니다.

어떻게 하면 일어나는 이 마음을 주인공 자리에 탁 맡겨 놓을 수 있는지, 큰스님의 큰 가르침 부탁드립니다.

큰스님: 여기 앉아 계신 분들 중에도 댁 같은 일을 겪는 분이 많이 계실 거라고 생각이 됩니다. 물론 다 그런 경우는 아니지만 이거는 댁의 약한 마음을 고치시기만 하면 됩니다.

애초에 본인의 신념을 믿고 끌고 가면 되는데 마음이 약해 이 사람 저 사람 말을 믿고 가니 문제가 생기죠. 그런 사람들의 말을 100% 믿지는 않았더라도 그래도 믿고 가는 부분이 있으니 문제가 된 거예요.

goes on, the money I owe is increasing. I've been raising and entrusting the thought that, "Only my foundation, my true essence, can solve this problem."

However, worries still sometimes overwhelm me. Kun Sunim, please tell me how I can completely let go of these worries.

Kun Sunim: I think there are many people here who have experienced something similar. Every case is different, of course, but for you, things will be fine if you can just strengthen your trust in your foundation. You should have been doing things from a position of strong faith, but because your faith wavers easily, you listened to people you shouldn't have.

You didn't get mindlessly drawn into what they said, but you did believe some of it. Which led to the problems you're in. No matter what you encounter, your true self is what you need to be looking to for guidance, and where you should be asking your questions. If you're looking to others instead, only trouble will follow.

Of course, getting cheated exists there within the functioning of the truth, as does avoiding

어떤 일이라도 내면의 자기한테 물어봐야지 딴 사람한테 물어봐서는 해결이 되지 않습니다. 물론 남한테 당하는 것도 부처님 법이고 당하지 않는 것도 부처님 법이지만 일이 잘못되면 본인이 힘들잖아요. 그러니까 그런 일을 안 겪으려면 미리 '나쁜 일을 당하지 않게 너만은 할 수 있잖아.' 하고 단단히 안에다 넣어야죠.

그렇게 자기 근본에 그것부터 꽝 집어넣고 가면 나쁜 일이 생길 곳에는 가기 싫어지고 그런 사람하고도 같이 일하기 싫어져요.

그러니깐 댁의 경우는 마음이 약해서 그렇게 됐다고 생각하시고, 요 다음에는 제 3자를 이번처럼 철석같이 믿지는 마세요. 다른 사람이 하는 말을 듣기는 하되, 100% 믿지는 마십시오.

같이 일을 하는 사람을 아끼되 속으로 아끼시구요. 그 사람도 나쁘게 만들 필요가 없습니다.

being cheated; but one will cause you hardships and suffering, so it's better to avoid it. So, before you begin something, entrust the thought that, "Only you, my foundation, can protect me from harmful things." If you entrust a firm thought like this, you'll naturally feel an aversion to locations that won't work out or people who will lead to trouble.

Next time, you need to be more firm in how you raise thoughts like these. Also, don't be so quick to completely believe what others are telling you. I'm not saying to distrust them. Trust them, care for them, but don't lose sight of your foundation.

Be careful about making people into favorites, and even if you feel like someone cheated you, don't make them into something bad or evil. Behaviors like these are why your business problem happened. They created an atmosphere ripe for gossiping and scheming, which, without you being aware of it, gave rise to the problems that caused your bankruptcy.

So, next time, be more careful, and start by firmly entrusting the thought to your foundation that, "It's you that can make this business go

여러 사람이 소곤소곤하기만 하고 댁은 아무것도 모르니 일이 그렇게 벌어진 거에요. 그러니까 요 다음에는 그렇게 하지 마시고 시작할 때도 '너만이 할 수 있어.' 하고 확실하게 매듭을 짓고 시작하고 마무리할 때도 확실하게 하세요. 처음 시작뿐만 아니라 그 끄트머리에 가서 회향(回向)[11]할 때가 제일 어렵지 않습니까? 그 회향 끄트머리에 할 것까지 결정을 짓고 하세요.

질문자 4(남): 저는 부산 지원 법형제회에서 공부하고 있습니다. 이렇게 질문할 수 있도록 마음 내 주신 모든 분들께 감사드립니다.

첫 번째 질문입니다. 큰스님 법문에 어느 사람이 길을 가다가 보니까 자기 형제가 소가 되어 서 있었는데 얼른 자기의 가죽 주머니에 넣어서 형제는 자기가 되었다는 말씀이 있습니다.

---

11. 회향(回向): 자신이 닦은 선근(善根), 공덕(功德)을 '참나'인 주인공에 돌려 놓으며, 또한 다른 이들에게 그 감사함을 되돌리어 더불어 함께 깨달음을 이루게 한다는 뜻. 일체가 공용, 공식하며 돌아가고 있으니 나 혼자 무엇을 했다 할 수 없고, 밥 한 그릇을 먹어도 우주 만물에 감사하지 않을 수 없음을 알아, 그 감사함과 공덕을 모두에게 돌리는 것을 의미함.

well." You also need to be sure to raise this kind of thought about finishing things well. And when you finish, there's all kinds of reasons why it's hard to give something back, aren't there? So, before you even begin, make a firm decision to give something back when you finish.

Questioner 4 (male): Thank you for this opportunity to ask you a question. During one of your Dharma talks, you told us the story of a man who was walking along a road when he encountered a cow. As soon as he saw the cow, he suddenly understood that this was his brother, reborn. So he put his brother's spirit within his own body and became one with him.

You then asked us to do this when we encounter beings we have a prior connection with, who have been reborn in unfortunate circumstances. We should absorb them into our foundation and live together. But, and this is my question, how does this work? It almost sounds like what shamans and psychics do, when they invite a spirit into their body so that they can use its ability.

큰스님께서는 이와 같이 인연되는 불쌍한 생명들을 자신의 근본자리에 흡수하라고 말씀하셨는데, 이렇게 흡수해서 살아가는 것과 무당이 귀신을 불러서 점도 치고 하면서 영(靈)과 함께 살아가는 것과는 분명하게 차이가 있다고 생각이 듭니다. 그렇긴하지만 좀 더 확실히 알고 싶어서 질문 드립니다.

큰스님: 내 주인공 자리는 남이 볼 때에 있는 것도 아니고 없는 것도 아닙니다. 이건 말로 표현할 수가 없는 자리입니다.

그래서 공부하는 도반(道伴)[12]들끼리는 '너는 귀신 방귀씨를 얻었느냐? 얻었으면 공치기할 공마당은 만들어놨느냐?'라는 소리도 하는 겁니다. 이 자리는 귀신을 만 명을 넣었다 하더라도 넣은 사이가 없고 만 명을 여기서 꺼냈다 하더라도 꺼낸 사이가 없습니다. 아까 어느 박사님이 수술에 대해 얘기하셨는데, 만약 환자가 100명이라면 내 주인공이 그 100명에게 다 들어가서 수술을 하고도 남습니다. 그러니까 그렇게 들어가도 들어간 사이가 없고, 나가도 나간 사이가 없고,

---

12. 도반(道伴): 함께 도(道)를 닦는 벗

Kun Sunim: As for how it works, when it comes to your Juingong, it clearly exists, yet whether others perceive it or not depends upon the depth of their own practice. So, sometimes practitioners would test each other, saying things like, "Have you grasped the seed of a ghost's fart?[11] If you have, are you able to go out and play with a ball?"[12]

Even though you put 10,000 ghosts into this foundation, they become one with our foundation in an instant. Even though you send forth 10,000 beings from this place, it happens in an instant. Earlier, a doctor asked about surgery, right? If there were one hundred people needing surgery, your foundation could easily manifest one hundred invisible doctors that would enter them and perform the surgeries. This is how your foundation works: instantly, entering and leaving, taking things in or out, and doing it all without leaving any trace.

---

11. Here, a "ghost's fart" is a way of saying "nothing."

12. In Korean, the word for "ball" is a homophone with "emptiness."

꺼내도 꺼낸 사이가 없고, 넣어도 넣는 사이가 없습니다.

예전에 이 공부를 못해서 아주 처참하게 사셨고 활현(活現)을 못하신 부모님과 조상님들이 계신 집들이 있으시죠? 그런데 만약 여러분들 중에 지금 자손들의 몸이 있으니까 함께 공부하셔야 될 텐데 하는 마음이 있다면 그렇게 하세요. 그 조상들이 자손의 마음에 들어가도 자손에게 절대로 해가 되지 않습니다. 들어간 사이 없이 들어가 있고 배우는 사이 없이 배우고 자식이 배우는 대로 배우고 또 나가도 나가는 사이 없이 활현하시고 그럽니다. 또 만약에 조상이 그럴 마음이 있어 그걸 자손에게 알리려 한다든가 한다면 꿈으로라도 연상이 되겠죠. 그러니까 모두 그게 좋은 일이니까 그걸 무서워서 쩔쩔 매고 해결을 못해 쩔쩔 매고 이러지 마세요. 그런다면 어떻게 진정한 사람이라고 할 수 있습니까?

우리는 지금 수없는 세월을 거쳐 진화해 짐승의 모습을 다 벗고 나와 사람이 된 겁니다. 또 사람이 된 후라도 사람으로 살던 습을 다 놔야만 승천에 오르죠. 그래야 더불어 같이 사는 공식(共食)으로서의 내가 자유자재권을 가지고 살 수 있죠.

Among you, there are probably people who had parents or ancestors who didn't know about spiritual practice, and who also lived hard, brutal lives. If it occurs to you that it would be good for those spirits to practice together with you, then invite them to join you. Even though they combine with you, they won't cause you any problems at all. Likewise, they'll leave no traces behind as they learn, nor as they leave to be reborn. If they want to tell you something about what's going on with them, they may do it through dreams or something similar.

You might be scared or unsettled by what you experience, but don't be, because practicing together like this is good for everyone involved. By shedding one shape after another for eons, you've already evolved to the point where you can have a human body. So don't let yourself be scared by those kinds of things; that's not the path to becoming a true human being.

Having come this far, we have to dissolve the habits of this level as well. Only then can we reach higher levels and truly live as one with others, having the ability to solve any problem we come across.

질문자 4: 두 번째 질문은 저의 체험담입니다. 작년 초에 호흡이 잘 되지 않아서 잠을 자다가도 깨고, 앉아 있어도 힘든 경우가 이따금씩 계속되었습니다.

그래서 약국에서 청심환을 사 먹어도 그때뿐이고 병원에 가서 심전도를 비롯한 여러 가지 검사를 해 봐도 특별한 이상이 없다 하여 한의원에서 약을 먹고 지냈습니다. 그리고 얼마간 괜찮았는데 다시 이런 상태가 계속되었습니다. 그러면서 주인공에게 '너만이 할 수 있다.'고 관하였으나 한편으로는 병원에 가서 정밀검사를 받지 않고 그대로 두어도 괜찮을까 하는 불안한 생각도 떠올랐습니다.

그러던 어느 날 사무실에서 큰스님 법문 테이프를 듣고 있었는데 법문 내용 중에 '내가 아프더라도 어떻게 되어서 잘못되지는 않을까 하고 불안해하지 말고 죽든지 살든지 그 자리에 맡겨 놓으라.' 하는 말씀이 있었습니다.

Questioner 4: My second question is about my own experience, and whether there are any aspects of it I need to handle better.

Late last year, I began to have some difficulties breathing. This often woke me up during the night, so I really wasn't sleeping well, either. I found some medicine that helped me breathe better, but as soon as I stopped taking it, the problem returned.

I went to the hospital, but the doctors there said that I was fine. So I went to an oriental medicine clinic, and those treatments worked for a while. But within a few months the problem returned. Then I remembered something you said, and raised the thought that, "Only you, my true essence, can make me healthy," and entrusted it to my foundation. Still, I was afraid, and thought that perhaps I should go to a bigger hospital for in-depth testing.

In the meantime, I'd gotten some cassette tapes of your teachings, and was listening to them. You said, "Even though you are sick, don't be worried about possible bad things that might happen. Have firm faith in your foundation and

이 말씀을 듣는 순간 불안한 생각이 사라지고 내가 만약 주인공을 믿는다면 주인공이 다 할 거라고 생각되어지면서 병원에 가지 않고 고칠 것이라면 그렇게 하고 병원에 가서 해결할 것이라면 누구를 시켜서라도 나를 병원에 가게 할 것이라는 확신이 생기고 마음이 편안해졌습니다.

그때가 점심 식사 후라서 노곤해 소파에서 이삼십 분 정도 잠을 자고 깨었는데 기분이 매우 상쾌하였고 자세히 모르지만 이상하게 제 몸이 가뿐하게 느껴졌습니다. 퇴근 후 지하철로 집에 올 때까지나 그 날 밤에 잘 때도 괜찮았고 그 후 4~5개월 정도 지난 지금까지 괜찮습니다. 이 점에 대해서 큰스님께 점검을 좀 받고 싶습니다.

큰스님: 그것뿐이 아닙니다. 아까 임신으로 인해 어려움을 겪는 사람들 애기도 들으셨지 않습니까?

entrust it with all of your anxieties and fears. Just go forward trusting it, regardless of whether you live or die."

When I heard this, the unrest within me suddenly disappeared. I felt very deeply that if I firmly relied upon my foundation, then it would take care of things and show me the way. If my condition were something that could be fixed without a doctor, then that would happen. And if I needed to see a doctor, then my foundation would lead me to a hospital.

I felt very confident in this, and the stress and tension in me drained away. This happened shortly after lunch, and I began to feel drowsy and took a nap. I slept for 20 minutes or so, and when I awoke, I felt really good. Ever since then, I've felt great, and have had no problems breathing. Is there anything I've overlooked or need to do differently going forward?

Kun Sunim: That's not all. You heard earlier of all the difficulties and dangers that pregnant women can experience, right? You all have a body that experiences all kinds of suffering as well, don't you? I do, too, because I have a body.

여러분들이 다 사람입니다. 나도 사람이고요. 그런데 이 사람의 모습이 나를 이끌고 살게 하는 게 아니라 내 근본이, 내 주인공이 내 모습을 살리는 겁니다. 내면에 자기 모습을 살리는 선장이 있습니다. 부처님께서 이걸 배로 비유해서 이야기한 것이 있죠.

파도에 휩쓸리고 이리저리 떠밀려 배가 요동을 쳐서 사람들이 그냥 아우성을 치고 야단들인데 그중 한 사람이 진정으로 자기 근본을 믿고 가만히 앉아 있었더니 파도가 잔잔해지고 전부 괜찮아지더라는 겁니다.

자기가 자기를 안 믿으면 누굴 믿습니까? 이 세상 누굴 믿어요? 지금 석가모니 부처님이 여러분 옆에 앉아 계신다해도 응해 주시는 것은 여러분들의 마음에 달린 겁니다. 여러분이 정말 넉넉하게 생각을 한다면 정말 넉넉하게 활용을 해 주시고 여러분이 그렇지 않게 생각할 때는 그렇지 않게 되는 거죠.

However, it's not this body that causes us to live, but rather our true self that enables our bodies to live. It is the captain within you that sustains and guides your flesh. The Buddha, too, once talked about this, using the metaphor of a ship. A storm arose, with wind and waves, and tossed a ship about. The people on board began to panic and cry, but there was one person who stayed calm and entrusted the situation to his foundation. As he did this, the waves became calm and the winds died away.

You have to believe in yourself! Of all the people and things in this world, you as your true self are what you have to believe in! Even if Buddha were sitting right here, whether he becomes one with you and works together with you would depend upon your mind. If your thoughts are generous and broad-minded, then Buddha will work together with you generously and compassionately. Whether this happens or not depends upon your thoughts.

If you work hard at raising kind and generous thoughts, even though difficulties and terrifying things happen, they won't be able to touch your heart, for the thoughts you give rise to manifest

그러니까 여러분들이 생각을 잘 하면 조금도 어려울 것도 없고 무서울 것도 없는 겁니다. 여러분들이 생각한 것이 항상 거죽으로 나오게 돼 있거든요. 아무리 안 그렇다고 해도 사람이 속으로부터 거죽으로 나오지 거죽으로부터 속으로 나오는 법은 없죠.

그러니깐 항상 그저 의연하고 웃고 살 수 있게 이미 지나간 것에 대한 생각을 하지 마시고 내일 생각을 하지 마세요. 살 생각을 말입니다. 살 생각을 하면 노냥 그거 생각을 해야 돼요. 여러분들의 습관에 의해 고통을 받는 것도 많습니다. 걱정하는 것이 습관이 되면요 걱정하지 않을 것도 걱정을 하거든요. 그러니까 될 수 있으면, 걱정하지 마시고 웃고 사세요.

여러분들이 좀 웃으시게 재미있게 말을 못해 죄송합니다. 근데 우리는 아주 재미있게 살 수 있는데 왜 재미있게 못 살까요? 이건 우리가 존재함으로써 생기는, 상대적인 관계에서 벌어지는 모든 일들 때문에 그렇지 않은가 싶습니다.

into the world. Everything in the world begins with our thoughts, and those thoughts always begin within us.

Thus, if you want to go forward in your life unbowed and with a smile, don't cling to yesterday's things, nor worry about what will come tomorrow, nor even about living itself. If you start dwelling on these things, they will become the focus of all your thoughts, and leave room for little else.

Much of your suffering comes from your habits, and if you keep worrying, that, too, will become a habit. You'll be worried and stressed over things you don't need to be concerned about. So, as much as possible, let go of your worries and live with a smile and a laugh.

I feel a little bad that my Dharma talks are so serious, and don't give you much of a chance for a good laugh. We are all fully capable of living with joy and laughter, so why aren't we? Because we exist, we encounter all kinds of different experiences and problems, but all of those can be solved by viewing them wisely and entrusting that to our foundation.

그렇지만 알고 보면 모두가 한생각[13]에 불과해요. 산이나 들이나 이런 자연에서도 문제가 생기는데 그런 것도 한생각에 다 완화가 되고 한생각에 그냥 뒤집어지고 하는 거죠. 여러분들이 이 한생각을 잘 하시면 산에 오르고 내리다가도 잘 얻어먹고 잘 자고 내려오시게 돼요.

질문자 4: 스님, 감사합니다.

큰스님: 참 알아듣기 쉽게 말을 잘 해드려야 할 텐데 내가 말을 잘 못해서 미안한 점이 많습니다. 하지만 말을 못하는 걸 어떡합니까? (대중 웃음)

질문자 5(남): 감사합니다 큰스님. 저는 본원의 법형제회에서 공부하고 있습니다. 시간이 많이 됐으니 간단히 말씀드리겠습니다.

---

13. 한생각: 어떤 생각을 우리 내면의 근본자리에 입력시키거나 맡겨놓았을 때, 근본을 통해 나오는 생각은 우리 몸속의 모든 생명들뿐만 아니라 이 세상의 만물만생에 전달되며, 일체가 그 생각에 응하게 됨. 보이지 않는 정신계, 즉 우리 근본마음을 통해 일으켜지는 생각은 물질계에서 현실로 나타나게 됨. 이렇게 근본을 통해 나오게 되는 생각을 한생각이라 함.

Even with problems of the natural world, the thoughts we give rise to can solve those, or make them much worse. This is why I'm always saying you have to be careful in how you raise thoughts. Even while deep in the mountains, if you raise a thought wisely, you will be given food and shelter.

Questioner 5 (male): It's wonderful to see you like this, but I see that we are behind schedule, so I'll be brief.

Kun Sunim: Relax, and sit comfortably. Even if someone tries to hit you with a stick, you need to be able to remain unshaken and do what you came for.

Questioner 5: Thank you. First, I'd like to ask you about a dream I had a few days ago. You showed up in my dream, affectionately stroked my head as if I were a small child, saying, "Tomorrow is my birthday," and left. In my dream, I wanted to buy you a cake, and was about to go order a three-tier cake for you. At that point, I woke up, and have been wondering about this dream ever since.

큰스님: 편히 앉아서 하세요. 누가 방망이로 친다 하더라도 좀 안정되게 앉아서 할 수 있는 그 마음이 필요합니다.

질문자 5: 예 감사합니다. 간단히 두 가지만 질문드리겠습니다. 며칠 전에 꿈인지 생신지 비몽사몽간에 큰스님이 제 머리를 쓰다듬으시면서 "내일이 내 생일이다."라고 말씀하시고는 가셨습니다. 그래서 제가 꿈속에서도 '그럼 내일 큰스님한테 3단 케이크를 주문해다가 드려야 되겠다.'고 생각하고 그걸 주문하러 가려고 하는데 꿈이 깨 버렸습니다. 그게 무슨 뜻인지 설명해 주시면 감사하겠습니다.

큰스님: 하하하하하하. 그래 3단 케이크라는 것은 보기에도 멋있어서 즐거운 마음으로 잘 먹을 수 있는 거 아닙니까? 근데 생일이라고 나한테 준다고 그랬단 말입니다. 댁에서 어저께도 살았고 내일도 살고 오늘도 사는데 오늘 사는 게 공했으니까 그저 둘 아니게 할 수 있는 마음이 있으면, 3단을 한데 합쳐서 항상 함이 없이 넣고 꺼내고 그렇게 하시고 살면 좀 지혜가 많이 생기겠죠.

Kun Sunim: [Laughs.] Thank you! But instead of giving me that cake, you should be able to eat and enjoy it yourself. Now, the three tiers: You lived yesterday, you will live tomorrow, and you're living now, but all of those form one ceaselessly flowing whole. If you can view all things nondualistically, and if you can do everything from this foundation, while letting go of any trace of "me" or "I," then great wisdom will arise.

Questioner 5: Thank you. Second, I'd like to ask you about a thought that arose within me: "Within me questions are asked without speaking, and answered without speaking. But they are both still one. Why is this?"

Kun Sunim: We're functioning like that right now, aren't we? Within us right now, speaking, answering, giving, and receiving are all happening as one flowing whole. However, to truly realize this for yourself, you need to be the one to eat that cake, instead of trying to give it to me.

질문자 5: 감사합니다. 두 번째는, 하나 안에서 말없이 질문하는 것이 있고 또 말없이 대답하는 것이 있습니다. 그런데도 역시 하나입니다. 이 무슨 연고인지 말씀 부탁드리겠습니다.

큰스님: 지금 그렇게 하고 있지 않습니까? 지금 하고 있는데요 뭐. 이게 말이 없이 말을 한다, 또 대답 없이 대답을 한다, 주는 거 없이 주는 걸 받는다, 이런 것이 다 요소가 있습니다.

좀 전에 얘기했지만 3단 케이크를 해서 드린다 이럴 때 나에게 주는 게 아니라 댁에서 그걸 먹어야 되겠죠. 그러면 부모 조상님들까지 다 잡숫겠죠.

질문자 5: 감사합니다. 두 번째까지 질문은 끝났는데요 오늘 이 자리에서 한마디 더 하고 싶습니다. 오늘은 네 사람만 질문을 하게 되어 있어서 시간상 못 할 줄 알았는데 이렇게 기회가 주어져서 너무 감사합니다. 오늘 질문을 할 수 있을 거라 믿었습니다.

To put it another way, you need to take everything that arises and feed it back to your foundation. When you can do this, all of your parents and ancestors will be connected there and share in that cake together.

Questioner 5: Thank you. When I lined up to ask you a question, I was the fifth person, and was told that only four people could ask questions today because of the time. But I firmly raised the thought that I wanted to ask you my questions, and it turned out so.

Kun Sunim: Yes, go forward like that.

Sometimes people tend to give up before even trying, don't they? Just the other day, a man said to me, "This thing I have to do will fail anyway; there's no point in even raising a positive thought. It's such a bad situation that I don't know why I'm even bothering you with it."

So I said to him, "That which you think is possible or not is nothing more than your own guesses and habits of thinking. Leave all those behind! The truth of what the Buddha taught is having faith in the great interconnected energy

큰스님: 예. 그렇게 하세요. 어떤 사람들은 일을 하기도 전에 미리 '이거는 해봤자 안 되잖아.'라고 생각합니다. 예전에 한 사람이 "이거는 아무리 해도 안 되는 거기 때문에 관하지도 않습니다."라면서 "스님한테도 얘기할 수가 없습니다." 이러는 겁니다.

그래서 "이 부처님 법이라는 진리는 내가 이렇게 살아오면서 습관으로 알고 배우는 걸 말하는 게 아니고, 할 수 있다 할 수 없다 이걸 떠나서, 모든 걸 자기 근본이 한다는 걸 믿고 그냥 결정을 짓는 것이다."라고 했어요.

여러분들에게 무슨 급한 일이 생길 때, 예를 들어 다급한 일이 벌어져 회사가 부도나면 다 죽는다 할 때도 내 한생각이 결정적이면 그건 일단 멈춰집니다. 일단 그렇게 멈춰 놓고 그러고 더 큰 손해를 보지 않도록 노력해야죠.

하여튼 여러분들이 이 도리를 알고 가야 됩니다. 내가 살다 보니깐 여러분들이 이 도리를 꼭 알아야겠다 싶어서 자꾸 말씀을 드리는 거에요.

요새 시대로는 맞지 않는 소리일 수도 있겠지만 내가 이번 생에 여자로 태어나 살다 보니 이 세상에 너무 많은 여자들이 이 도리를 몰라서 울기도 많이 울고 스스로 목숨도 많이

and flowing of everything, and then deciding, from this very deep place, which way things need to go."

When something very urgent arises, like if your company is about to go bankrupt, then firmly decide how you need things to go, and entrust that to your foundation. In this way, you can prevent the situation from getting worse, and gain time to minimize the damage.

Anyway, you all should deeply understand this principle. I meet a lot of people every day, and see how important it is that everyone understands this. That's why I keep talking about it.

My experiences may seem like something from another age to young people today, but having lived as a woman, I've met so many women who led desperately unhappy and unfortunate lives because they were unaware of this ability within them. Some of them even took their own lives. Many others wanted to be reborn as men in their next lives because of their suffering. I haven't always been born as a woman, but this time I chose to be born with a plain-looking, female shape. A very plain shape was needed to accomplish my goal.

끊고 하더라고요. 그래서 남자로 태어나 살고 싶어 했던 여자들이 많았습니다. 저도 쭉 여자로만 살았던 건 아니지만 이번엔 이렇게 못생긴 여자로 나왔습니다. 못생기게, 아주 못생기게 나와야, 끝까지 잘 회향하고 갈 수 있는 상황이었으니까요. 그러니까 누구를 봐도 잘 생겼다 못 생겼다 하는 건 중요하지 않아요.

여러분들은 오직 그저 '나를 이끌고 가는 선장을 믿어야겠다.' 이렇게 꼭 생각을 하세요. '나를 이끌고 다니는 이 선장이 제일이다. 내 선장은 급하면 이렇게도 화하고 저렇게도 화해서 나를 이끌어 준다.'라고요. 내 선장에게 모든 걸 믿고 맡기면 나뿐만 아니라 나한테 결부된 사람들은 다 이끌게 돼 있어요.

몇 해 전에 어느 분이 와서 그래요. "스님, 형제들이 막 싸워서 집안이 그냥 다 망하다시피 했는데 우리 집안을 좀 살리려면 어떻게 하면 좋을까요?"라는 겁니다.

그런데 지금도 이 도리를 모르는 분들이 많지만, 그 전에는 신도님들이 훨씬 더 몰랐을 때니까 어떻게 했으면 좋을까를 말로 해줘서 될 일이 아니지 않습니까? 그래서 천상 심부름을 해도 아래 위 심부름꾼인 내가 해야 하니깐

You need to think like this: "I believe in the captain, my true self, who is guiding me. This captain is the best. When the situation is urgent, this captain manifests in all kinds of different ways to take care of me." This is important; whether you are good looking or not just isn't. When you have this kind of firm faith in your foundation and entrust everything to it, it will guide and take care of not only you, but also the people in your life that you are close to.

A few years ago a man came here and asked me a question: "My brothers and I have been having horrible fights, with people even hitting each other and throwing things. We have to get together for various family memorial services, and this fighting has just about destroyed our family. What can I do to change this?"

Even these days, there are many people here who don't understand this truth of their fundamental mind, but back in those days there were many more who didn't understand it. Well, I could see that even though I told him exactly what to do, he wouldn't be able to follow through with that. I realized that I would have to be the one to run this errand between the seen and unseen

알겠노라고 그냥 그러고 말았습니다만 그 후에 그 집 형제들이 전부 화해를 하고 더 이상 작대기를 가지고 죽인다 안 죽인다 하며 싸우지 않게 되었답니다. 그리고 지금까지 잘 산답니다.

그러니 여러분들이 지금 사시는데 고통스럽더라도 한 생을 공부해서 세세생생을 얻어야 되겠다는 마음을 좀 더 내어야겠습니다.

내가 자식들을 거죽만 귀엽다고 생각했지 세세생생에 어디로 굴러서 어떤 모습으로, 어떤 차원으로 어떻게 살건지 그런 거는 한 번도 생각해 보지 못하고 살지 않습니까? 그리고 자기 부모가 저 쪽에서 살다가 이 쪽으로 와서 내 자식으로 태어났는데도 모르잖아요. 그런데 공부를 하지 않으면 어떡하십니까?

그러니까 누구든지 자식이 되었든 부모가 되었든 상대를 우습게 생각하지 마세요. 남의 영가(靈駕)도 마찬가지 입니다.

realms. So I told him, "I understand, I'll do my job," and he left feeling much relieved. A while later, I heard that the brothers had reconciled, and that the whole family had become much more harmonious.

Even though your life is tough right now, you have to practice diligently so that you can do these kinds of things for yourself. Practice during this one life such that the benefits of that will last across all your future lives. Practice such that you will forever be able to live freely, and freely make use of the great ability inherent within you.

Everyone here loves and cares for their children, but have you ever thought about where your children are headed after this life? Have you ever wondered about what path their future lives will take? What shape they'll have, what spiritual level they'll be living at? Even when those who were once your parents are reborn as your own children, you can't see this, can you? So, don't look down upon anyone, not your parents, not your children, not anyone. Nor even upon those who have passed away.

광명선원뿐만 아니라 영탑이 있는 데는 일년에 한 번씩이라도 스님들이 직접 관여해서 영탑을 닦아내고 씻어내어서 말갛게 내 부모 탑처럼 해 놓습니다. 그 탑에 모셔져 있는 분들이 누굽니까? 남이 아닙니다. 그렇게 하는 게 스님들 잘 살려고 하는 게 아니죠.

이렇게 나, 너 분별하지 않고 모두 다 내 근본자리에 넣어 하나가 됨으로써 우리는 세세생생을 얻습니다. 우리 더불어 같이 세세생생을 얻읍시다.

Some of our centers have stupa parks for deceased family members and ancestors, don't they? The sunims there clean and wash the stupas once a year, as if they were their own. Who are those people in the stupas? They aren't strangers. The sunims aren't doing this for the money.

When we let go of distinctions between ourselves and others, becoming one with them all as we entrust them, and "me," to our foundation, we will attain the great way and be able to live freely, life after life. We will be able to use the infinite ability within each of us to help whoever is in need. Let's all do this together!

한마음출판사의 마음을 밝혀주는 도서

- A Thousand Hands of Compassion
  만가지 꽃이 피고 만가지 열매 익어
  :대행큰스님의 뜻으로 푼 천수경 (한글/영어)
  [2010 iF Communication Design Award 수상]
- Wake Up And Laugh (영어)
- No River To Cross, No Raft To Find (영어)
- It's Hard To Say (영어) (절판)
- My Heart Is A Golden Buddha (영어)
- Touching The Earth (영어)
- 생활 속의 참선수행 (시리즈) (한글/영어)
  1. 죽어야 나를 보리라
     (To Discover Your True Self, "I" Must Die)
  2. 함이 없이 하는 도리
     (Walking Without A Trace)
  3. 맡겨놓고 지켜봐라
     (Let Go And Observe)
  4. 마음은 보이지 않는 행복의 창고
     (Mind, Treasure House Of Happiness)
  5. 일체를 용광로에 넣어라
     (The Furnace Within Yourself)
  6. 온 우주를 살리는 마음의 불씨
     (The Spark That Can Save The Universe)
  7. 한마음의 위력
     (The Infinite Power Of One Mind)
  8. 일체를 움직이는 그 자리
     (In The Heart Of A Moment)

9. 한마음 한뜻이 되어
      (One With The Universe)
   10. 지구보존
      (Protecting The Earth)
   11. 진짜 통하게 되면
      (Inherent Connections, 2016 new)
   12. 잘 돼야 돼!
      (Finding A Way Forward, 2016 new)
   13. 콩씨를 믿는 콩싹
      (Faith In Action, 2016 출판예정)

- 내 마음은 금부처 (한글)
- 건널 강이 어디 있으랴 (한글)
- 처음 시작하는 마음공부1 (한글) (2016 출판예정)
- El Camino Interior (스페인어)
- Vida De La Maestra Seon Daehaeng (스페인어)
- Enseñanzas De La Maestra Daehaeng (스페인어)
- Práctica Del Seon En La Vida Diaria (Colección) (스페인어/영어)
   1. Una Semilla Inherente Alimenta El Universo
      (The Spark That Can Save The Universe)
- Si Te Lo Propones, No Hay Imposibles (스페인어)
- 人生不是苦海 (번체자 중국어) (개정판)
- 无河可渡 (간체자 중국어)
- 我心是金佛 (간체자 중국어) (개정판)

외국출판사에서 출판된 한마음도서

- Wake Up And Laugh
  Wisdom Publications, 미국

- No River To Cross
  (*No River To Cross, No Raft To Find* 영어판)
  Wisdom Publications, 미국

- Wie Flieβendes Wasser
  (*My Heart Is A Golden Buddha* 독일어판)
  Goldmann Arkana-Random House, 독일

- Ningún Río Que Cruzar
  (*No River To Cross* 스페인어판)
  Kailas Editorial, S.L., 스페인

- Umarmt Von Mitgefühl
  ('만가지 꽃이 피고 만가지 열매 익어':
  대행큰스님의 뜻으로 푼 천수경 독일어판)
  Diederichs-Random House, 독일

- 我心是金佛
  (*My Heart Is A Golden Buddha* 번체자 중국어판)
  橡樹林文化出版, 대만

- Vertraue Und Lass Alles Los
  (*No River To Cross* 독일어판)
  Goldmann Arkana-Random House, 독일

- Wache Auf Und Lache
  (*Wake Up And Laugh* 독일어판)
  Theseus, 독일

- Дзэн И Просветление
  (*No River To Cross* 러시아어판)
  Amrita-Rus, 러시아

- Sup Cacing Tanah
  (*My Heart Is A Golden Buddha* 인도네시아어판)
  PT Gramedia, 인도네시아

- Không có sông nào để vượt qua
  (*No River To Cross* 베트남어판)
  Phuong Nam Books, 베트남

- *No River To Cross*
  (*No River To Cross* 아랍어판, 제목미상)
  Sphinx Publishing, 이집트 (2016 출판예정)

Books by Daehaeng Kun Sunim
-available through Hanmaum Publications

- Touching The Earth (English) (2015 new)
- A Thousand Hands of Compassion (bilingual, Korean/English)
  [received **2010 iF communication design Award**]
- Wake Up And Laugh (English)
- No River To Cross, No Raft To Find (English)
- My Heart Is A Golden Buddha (English)
- One Mind: Principles (English) (Forthcoming 2016)
- *Practice in Daily Life* (Series) (bilingual, Korean/English)
  1. To Discover Your True Self, "I" Must Die
  2. Walking Without A Trace
  3. Let Go And Observe
  4. Mind, Treasure House Of Happiness
  5. The Furnace Within Yourself
  6. The Spark That Can Save The Universe
  7. The Infinite Power Of One Mind
  8. In The Heart Of A Moment
  9. One With The Universe
  10. Protecting The Earth
  11. Inherent Connections (2016 new)
  12. Finding A Way Forward (2016 new)
  13. Faith In Action (Forthcoming 2016)
- 건널 강이 어디 있으랴 (Korean)
- 내 마음은 금부처 (Korean)
- El Camino Interior (Spanish)
- Vida De La Maestra Seon Daehaeng (Spanish)

- Enseñanzas De La Maestra Daehaeng (Spanish)
- Práctica Del Seon En La Vida Diaria (Series) (bilingual, Spanish/English)
  1. Una Semilla Inherente Alimenta El Universo
- Si Te Lo Propones, No Hay Imposibles (Spanish)
- 人生不是苦海 (Traditional Chinese) (new edition)
- 无河可渡 (Simplified Chinese)
- 我心是金佛 (Simplified Chinese) (new edition)

-Books available through other Publishers

- No River To Cross
  Wisdom Publications, U.S.A.

- Wake Up And Laugh
  Wisdom Publications, U.S.A.

- Wie Fließendes Wasser
  German edition of *My Heart Is A Golden Buddha*
  Goldmann Arkana-Random House, Germany

- Vertraue Und Lass Alles Los
  German edition of *No River To Cross*
  Goldmann Arkana-Random House, Germany

- Umarmt Von Mitgefühl
  German edition of *A Thousand Hands Of Compassion*
  Diederichs-Random House, Germany

- Wache Auf Und Lache
  German edition of *Wake Up And Laugh*
  Theseus, Germany

- Ningún Río Que Cruzar
  Spanish edition of *No River To Cross*
  Kailas Editorial, S.L., Spain

- 我心是金佛
  Traditional Chinese edition of *My Heart Is A Golden Buddha*
  Oak Tree Publishing Co., Taiwan

- Дзэн И Просветление
  Russian edition of *No River To Cross*
  Amrita-Rus, Russia

- Sup Cacing Tanah
  Indonesian edition of *My Heart Is A Golden Buddha*
  PT Gramedia, Indonesia

- Không có sông nào để vượt qua
  Vietnam edition of *No River To Cross*
  Phuong Nam Books, Vietnam

- *No River To Cross* (*title to be determined*)
  Arabic edition of *No River To Cross*
  Sphinx Publishing, Egypt, Forthcoming 2016

한마음선원본원

경기도 안양시 만안구 경수대로1282 (석수동, 한마음선원)
(우편번호 13908)
Tel : 82-31-470-3100   Fax : 82-31-470-3116
홈페이지 : http://www.hanmaum.org
이메일 : jongmuso@hanmaum.org

국내지원

강릉지원 (우)25565 강원도 강릉시 하평5길 29(포남동)
   TEL:(033) 651-3003   FAX:(033) 652-0281

공주지원 (우)32522 충청남도 공주시 사곡면 위안양골길 157-61
   TEL:(041) 852-9100   FAX:(041) 852-9105

광명선원 (우)27638 충청북도 음성군 금왕읍 대금로1402
   TEL:(043) 877-5000   FAX:(043) 877-2900

광주지원 (우)61965 광주광역시 서구 운천로204번길 23-1(치평동)
   TEL:(062) 373-8801   FAX:(062) 373-0174

대구지원 (우)42152 대구광역시 수성구 수성로41길 76(중동)
   TEL:(053) 767-3100   FAX:(053) 765-1600

목포지원 (우)58696 전라남도 목포시 백년대로266번길 31-1(상동)
   TEL:(061) 284-1771   FAX:(061) 284-1770

문경지원 (우)36937 경상북도 문경시 산양면 봉서1길 10
   TEL:(054) 555-8871   FAX:(054) 556-1989

부산지원 (우)49113 부산광역시 영도구 함지로79번길 23-26(동삼동)
   TEL:(051) 403-7077   FAX:(051) 403-1077

울산지원 (우)44200 울산광역시 북구 달래골길 26-12(천곡동)
   TEL:(052) 295-2335   FAX:(052) 295-2336

제주지원 (우)63308 제주특별자치도 제주시 황사평6길 176-1(영평동)
TEL:(064) 727-3100   FAX:(064) 727-0302

중부경남 (우)50871 경상남도 김해시 진영읍 하계로35
TEL:(055) 345-9900   FAX:(055) 346-2179

진주지원 (우)52602 경상남도 진주시 미천면 오방로528-40
TEL:(055) 746-8163   FAX:(055) 746-7825

청주지원 (우)28540 충청북도 청주시 청원구 교서로109
TEL:(043) 259-5599   FAX:(043) 255-5599

통영지원 (우)53021 경상남도 통영시 광도면 조암길 45-230
TEL:(055) 643-0643   FAX:(055) 643-0642

포항지원 (우)37635 경상북도 포항시 북구 우창로59(우현동)
TEL:(054) 232-3163   FAX:(054) 241-3503

Anyang Headquarters of Hanmaum Seonwon

1282 Gyeongsu-daero, Manan-gu, Anyang-si,
Gyeonggi-do, 13908, Republic of Korea
Tel: (82-31) 470-3175 / Fax: (82-31) 470-3209
www.hanmaum.org/eng
onemind@hanmaum.org

Overseas Branches of Hanmaum Seonwon

ARGENTINA
Buenos Aires
Miró 1575, CABA, C1406CVE, Rep. Argentina
Tel: (54-11) 4921-9286 / Fax: (54-11) 4921-9286
www.hanmaum.org.ar

Tucumán
Av. Aconquija 5250, El Corte, Yerba Buena,
Tucumán, T4107CHN, Rep. Argentina
Tel: (54-381) 425-1400
www.hanmaumtuc.org

BRASIL
São Paulo
R. Newton Prado 540, Bom Retiro
Sao Paulo, CEP 01127-000, Brasil
Tel: (55-11) 3337-5291
www.hanmaumbr.org

CANADA
Toronto
20 Mobile Dr., North York, Ontario M4A 1H9, Canada
Tel: (1-416) 750-7943
http://www.hanmaum.org/IGateWeb/toronto/index.do

GERMANY
Kaarst
Broicherdorf Str. 102, 41564 Kaarst, Germany
Tel: (49-2131) 969551 / Fax: (49-2131) 969552
www.hanmaum-zen.de

THAILAND
Bangkok
86/1 Soi 4 Ekamai Sukhumvit 63
Bangkok, Thailand
Tel: (66-2) 391-0091
home.hanmaum.org/bangkok

USA
Chicago
7852 N. Lincoln Ave., Skokie, IL 60077, USA
Tel: (1-847) 674-0811
www.buddhapia.com/hmu/chi/

Los Angeles
1905 S. Victoria Ave., L.A., CA 90016, USA
Tel: (1-323) 766-1316
home.hanmaum.org/la

New York
144-39, 32 Ave., Flushing, NY 11354, USA
Tel: (1-718) 460-2019 / Fax: (1-718) 939-3974
www.juingong.org

Washington D.C.
7807 Trammel Rd., Annandale, VA 22003, USA
Tel: (1-703) 560-5166
http://home.hanmaum.org/wa

책에 관한 문의나 주문을 하실 분들은
아래의 연락처로 알려주십시오.

한마음국제문화원/한마음출판사

경기도 안양시 만안구 경수대로1282 (우)13908
전화: (82-31) 470-3175
팩스: (82-31) 470-3209
e-mail: onemind@hanmaum.org
www.hanmaumbooks.org

If you would like more information about these books or
would like to order copies of them,
please call or write to:

Hanmaum International Culture Institute
Hanmaum Publications
1282 Gyeongsu-daero, Manan-gu, Anyang-si,
Gyeonggi-do, 13908,
Republic of Korea
Tel: (82-31) 470-3175
Fax: (82-31) 470-3209
e-mail: onemind@hanmaum.org
www.hanmaumbooks.org